The Chosen One

Javier Macias

Unless otherwise noted, all scriptures are taken from the NEW INTERNATIONAL VERSION (NIV) Copyright© 1973, 1978, 1984, 1995, 1996, 1998, 2011, 2014 by Biblica, Inc.™. Used by permission of Zondervan

All scriptures with BOLD, UNDERLINED, ITALICIZED words or exclamation points are Author's Emphasis.

Scriptures marked AMP are taken from the AMPLIFIED® BIBLE, Copyright © 1954, 1958, 1962, 1964, 1965, 1987 by the Lockman Foundation Used by Permission. (www.Lockman.org)

Scriptures marked ERV are taken from the EASY TO READ VERSION – Copyright © 2006 by Bible League International

Scriptures marked GWT are taken from the GOD'S WORD TRANSLATION – Copyright © 1995 by God's Word to the Nations- used by permission of Baker Publishing Group

Scriptures marked GNB are taken from the GOOD NEWS BIBLE (GNB): Scriptures taken from the Good News Bible © 1994 published by the Bible Societies/HarperCollins Publishers Ltd UK, Good News Bible© American Bible Society 1966, 1971, 1976, 1992. Used with permission.

Scriptures marked NKJV are taken from the NEW KING JAMES VERSION (NKJV): Scripture taken from the NEW KING JAMES VERSION®. Copyright© 1982 by Thomas Nelson, Inc. Used by permission. All rights reserved.

Scriptures marked NLT are taken from the NEW LIVING TRANSLATION - Holy Bible, New Living Translation, copyright 1996, 2004, 2015 by Tyndale House Foundation. Used by permission of Tyndale House - Publishers Inc., Carol Stream, Illinois 60188. All Rights Reserved

Copyright © 2017 Javier Macias
All rights reserved.

ISBN-10: 1-946106-15-1
ISBN-13: 978-1-946106-15-5

Printed in USA. For Worldwide Distribution.

PUBLISHED BY:
Glorified Publishing
P.O. Box 8004
The Woodlands TX 77387
www.GlorifiedPublishing.com

DEDICATION

Dedicated to all of God's people who are wanting to know him more and becoming like him so "we the church" can become one. As the Father and son are one through the power of the Holy Spirit.

Jesus' Prayer (John 17).

CONTENTS

	ACKNOWLEDGMENTS	9
	INTRODUCTION	11
1	GOD'S CHOSEN ONE	13
2	SAMSON'S SECRET	15
3	SAMSON'S GIFT	29
4	SAMSON'S TEST	41
5	SAMSON'S FALL	51
6	SAMSON'S DEFEAT	61
7	SAMSON'S DEATH	71
8	A NEW BEGINNING	85
	ABOUT THE AUTHOR	91

ACKNOWLEDGMENTS

First and foremost I would like to acknowledge God my Father
in Heaven, for sharing with me revelations of his son Jesus Christ
through the power of the Holy Spirit.

I would also like to acknowledge my wife Polly Macias and my children
Samantha, Nikki, Thishalena, Javier Jr., Paulina, and Rosalina.
They have all stood by my side in preparing this book
for the people of God.

Introduction

We are on a mission to build an army of warriors for Christ, an army that can take back territory, as well as a lost generation of youth. With that goal in mind, we have written this book.

We are aiming to reach the youth of our society who have been literally mesmerized by the darkness of the kingdom of Satan in this society of ours. Many of them have contemplated suicide from divorce, sexual perversion, and violations of every type: sexual, physical, mental abuse, and bullying through social media.

This barely skims the surface of what our youth are up against. They have no solid foundation on which to stand in this very immoral and selfish, self-centered society that has lost touch with loving and caring for one another, Jesus Christ's greatest commandment.

That is why Satan has taken it upon himself to darken the minds, hearts, and souls of God's people.

We must get to where our Lord Jesus Christ needs us to be, in order to win back a generation that has literally been destroyed by the darkness of the kingdom of Satan. We are called to be the light of the world! Without Jesus Christ, there is no light in our darkened world. That is my position, as God's servant to his chosen people, with a passion for the youth of this nation.

Thus this book was born! This book will speak to the youth of today's culture in a way that no other can – through the heart and the mind of Jesus Christ, in TODAY'S language. As God speaks, and our "listener" answers Him, the reader will be ministered too, as well.

This book is NOT just for youth, however. It is also a healing balm for anyone who has ever encountered any kind of wounding or pain in his or her lifetime. This book will dig out all of that pain, show it to you and call it what it is. But it not only does that, it will help you to get rid of it, with the only possible solution: Jesus Christ.

So, now, I come as a light to you, my brothers and sisters in Christ, with God's calling on my life! Enjoy this work of the Holy Spirit!

"Then the Lord reached out his hand and touched my mouth and said to me, 'I have put my words in your mouth. See, today I appoint you over nations and kingdoms to uproot and tear down, to destroy and overthrow, to build and to plant.'" *(Jeremiah 1:9-10)*

"He said, 'Son of man, I AM *sending you to the Israelites, to a rebellious nation that has rebelled against me; they and their ancestors have been in revolt against me to this very day. The people to whom* I AM *sending you are obstinate and stubborn. Say to them, 'This is what the Sovereign Lord says.' And whether they listen or fail to listen- for they are a rebellious people- they will know that a prophet has been among them.'"* *(Ezekiel 2:3-4)*

CHAPTER ONE

God's Chosen One

The story of Samson and Delilah is one of power, strength, deception, defeat, and redemption. We all have, at one time in our lives, possessed and experienced all of those phases of life.

Power:
At one time in your life, everything was in your control and at your command. What you said went, and what you wanted you got, even if it went against other people's feelings and personal beliefs. You did as you pleased, even though it was not in your own best interests. You went against your own desires that are deep within you, the ones that give you happiness and joy, both to your soul, and to your being.

You were afraid of people making fun of you, and laughing at you. That's why you now have a generation of youth that has no respect towards others in their society, or even society itself.

Your parents cried, "You don't tell me how to discipline *my child*ren!" and "You can't discipline *my child*ren in school. Don't you lay a hand on *my child*! I will sue you!"

Even now, you still possess that power in your life that says what goes, and what doesn't, even though you don't get what you want all the time.

Yet, you still control your own, even when it's all wrong.

You say, "I do what I want, and no one tells me what to do!"

Strength:
We all have a will to live! There are many who feel life isn't worth living, because of negative people, injustice, sorry attitudes, and peer pressure all around. "Nobody cares anyway," they lament. This seems especially true when unexpected news of tragedy comes into one's life through a doctor's diagnosis, or a phone call from a family member of an unexpected death in the family.

Struggling economy… loss of jobs… divorce and crime in an evil society that has literally decayed in morality. Even when we reach within ourselves to make things right, they still turn out wrong. Regardless of what we do, when helping people, or helping family members and friends it seems they never show appreciation or gratitude of any kind toward our efforts.

Yet, we know there's got to be more than meets the eye!

Deception:
Who hasn't been lied to, or betrayed, by those we hold close to us? Who hasn't been taken advantage of? Even by those you would never expect it from, those who you thought were closest to you. It extends even into the political realm of our country that promises benefits, help, and assistance that one never receives. We have all been deceived, and lied to, at one time or another.

Defeat:
There isn't a soul on the face of the earth that has never suffered defeat in his life. Let downs! Disappointments! Failures! Hardships that affect every individual in humanity!

Death:
One doesn't need to literally die to experience death. To most of society overall, death is when one dies, and is laid to rest in his casket, followed by a funeral. At least for most people, this is what they think of as death.

As far as life itself is concerned, death according to the word of God is total separation from God. For most of humanity, we all have been there; some are there now, even as we speak. Having no experience of God's power and presence in our lives, we walk around because our physical body is alive, yet our inner soul being is as dead as one lying in a funeral parlor.

<u>Redemption:</u>
Conquering and overcoming: they are the total opposites of vengeance and retaliation. This is why millions fail to receive the happiness and peace this life has to offer for those who diligently do everything in a righteous way, keeping their hope alive through their faith in God.

So how is redemption obtained so that one may move on in life? How can one be set free from anger, resentment, unforgiveness, fear, hopelessness, and lack of trust, to name just a few of the evil spirits that manipulate millions of people lives?

Let's take a look into the story of Samson and Delilah. This story will have a drastic impact, changing your heart, soul, and mind towards life, helping you to win against all odds. After all, you are **God's chosen one**, created of him, to be like him in his image.

"Then God said, 'Let us make man in our image, in our likeness, and let them rule over the fish of the sea, and the birds of the air, over the livestock, over all the earth, and over all the creatures that move along the ground.' So God created man in his own image, in the image of God he created him; male and female he created them."   *(Genesis 1:26-27)*

"God blessed them and said to them, "Be fruitful and increase in number, fill the earth and subdue it. Rule over the fish of the sea and the birds of the air and over every living creature that moves on the ground."   *(Genesis 1:28)*

CHAPTER TWO

Samson's Secret

Can one really say they are blessed of God? Of course! That was a dumb question ... or was it? Not really!

I heard the Lord say, "Many of *my people* feel as though they have been left out when it comes to having special gifts and talents, even in their personal 'look' and appearance, showing out toward others in the life they live. That comes from *my people* going by what they see that makes them think that is what life is all about. In other words, most of you take life for granted, instead of thanking me daily for your blessings I do give you."

"Yes, the word was full of grace and truth, and from him, we all received one blessing after another."   *(John 1:16)*

"You have heard that it was said, "Love your neighbor and hate your enemy. "But I tell you, love your enemies and pray for those who persecute you, <u>that you may be children of your Father in heaven.</u> He causes his sun to rise on the evil and the good, and sends rain on the righteous and the unrighteousness."   *(Matthew 5:43-45)*

Then I heard the Lord say, "I, the Lord your God, brought that topic up because of everything that I see around me on a daily basis. Sin? Yes, it's bad, but it is not sin… it is the after effects of sin. If I sat here and named every sin that exists, I would never finish naming them. Anything contrary to My character, and my being as God (Holy) is sin. Including yourselves! That is why it is written,

"There is not one righteous, not even one." *(Romans 3:10)*

"For all have sinned and fall short of the Glory of God." *(Romans 3:23)*

"The after effects of sin have literally ruined millions upon millions of lives over the course of human history. Violent acts of murder, sexual perversion, drugs, alcohol drinking that leads to drunkenness, DWI'S that take out innocent lives on your byways and highways of travel, acts of greed, and so on. Those just mentioned would be labeled as visible sins, sins that are visible to the naked eye."

"Then you have the sins which are invisible to the naked eye, which are far worse in my eyes," says the Lord, "than those displayed in one's life, which are visible to the naked eye."

"He went on: What comes out of a man is what him 'unclean'! For from within, out of men's hearts come evil thoughts - sexual immorality, theft, murder, adultery, greed, malice, deceit, lewdness, envy, slander, arrogance and folly. All these evils come from inside and make a man unclean." *(Mark 7:20-23)*

"In the midst of this great darkness over your personal lives, and over you as a nation, beams a great light of hope and peace," says the Lord!"

"The light shines in the darkness, but the darkness has not understood it." *(John 1:5NIVR)*

"The darkness I speak of is the mind set of mankind in this United States of America! A nation that has been ruined over the years, leaving its people asking,

'Why did this happen to me? Why did this happen to us? What did I do wrong to deserve this? What did we, the people of this great country, do wrong to deserve what has happened over the years in our nation? I don't know if I will ever get over this, Lord! Will you help me, Lord? Will you help us as a nation? Do you even care, Lord?'"

"I will shed my great light into your darkened souls," says the Lord. "I will speak words of resurrection power into this United States of America, and to all *my people* who will accept My word and wholeheartedly believe it in their hearts," says the Lord.

"There was a man by the name of Zorah, named Manoah, from the clan of the Danites, had a wife who was childless, unable to give birth. The angel of the Lord appeared to her and said to her, You are barren and childless, but you are going to become pregnant and give birth to a Son. Now see to it that you drink no wine or other fermented drink and that you do not eat anything unclean. You will become pregnant and have a Son whose head is never to be touched by a razor because the boy is to be a Nazarite, dedicated to God from the womb. He will take the lead in delivering Israel from the hands of the Philistines." (Judges 13:2-5)

"America! You are about to give birth to *a Son*! My son, my daughter, you are about to give birth to *a Son*! You are going to see my love for you through my Son, Jesus Christ! My church, my body of believers, you have been barren and childless for too long! You are about to give birth to a Son!"

"The woman gave birth to a boy and named him Samson. He grew up and the Lord blessed him." (Judges 13:24)

"Samson was a chosen vessel of mine, the Lord your God, to help a nation be delivered from the hands, and the grip, of its enemy. I AM looking for my Samson in this very hour, who can change a nation, a country, a community, a city, a region, or even a family. But I must first help you, as an individual, change your own life and circumstances, in and around your own being as a person, or even as a nation this very day - before you can be effective to all others around you, and in your own life."

"I have chosen *you* to deliver *you* from the hands of your enemies," says the Lord! "Be it people, drugs, or drinking; sexual perversions, or loneliness; abuse, both physically and emotionally; broken heartedness, or whatever satan's hands are gripping you with by the throat, thus suffocating the life out of you."

"Really? I'm too far gone, Lord!"

"It doesn't matter! Don't ever under estimate me," says the Lord! "You will see my love for you when we finish this conversation TODAY! This very day, this very hour, down to this very moment, you will stand on my Word and my promise with your whole heart, soul and mind that tells you,

*'He chose us in him before the creation of the world to be holy and blameless in his sight, **IN CHRIST**.'"*   *(Ephesians 1:4)*

"First things first! Keep your mind on Christ, my Son, through this whole message, whether you feel worthy or not! This is about His power, and His Love for you in your life which far exceeds any love you have ever been given in this life of yours. This is about a love you never got from your earthly father or mother, who were too busy with their own selfish lives, living for themselves, and no one else.

"It also is a love that far exceeds any true loving mom or dad can give you as their child. It far exceeds the love you will get from a man or from a woman, even one you shared your whole life with, *until death did you part*. It will give you power in your life, unlimited power, even against all odds. This love you will experience today will have a force and a power in your life that you have never had before."

"Just do that much, as an act of faith, keeping your mind on Christ Jesus, my Son, and it is forever going to change your life. **TODAY** as you read the words, I, the Lord your God, will give to you as my promise, you will never think the same, or be the same for the rest of your life."

"I speak to you as a nation! I speak to you as an individual! I speak to you as my church, the body of Christ! Before he was even born, Samson was chosen of me, the Lord his God! I chose you, the United States of America, before you were ever born, says the Lord! I chose you, *my child*, before you were ever born! I chose you, my church before you were ever established!"

"The angel said, "The boy is to be a Nazirite, dedicated to God from the womb." *(Judges 13:5)*

"You were not only chosen of me before entering the womb, you were chosen of me before the foundations of the world were established," says the Lord! "I had you in my hands, America, before the creation of the world. I had you in my hands, *my child*, before the world was ever established."

"The womb is mentioned in the announcement for Samson's birth. There is no womb mentioned of you being chosen of me before the creation of the world in the book of Ephesians, chapter 1, verse 4. That means you are even more genuinely chosen of me, the Lord your God, to have you exist before you were ever in the womb. You should take that thought to heart, America! You should take that thought of me, the Lord your God, towards *you, my child*!"

"Very specific instructions were given about Samson's dedication to God. The angel specifically stated,

'His head is never to be touched by a razor.' *(Judges 13:5)"*

"His hair would be the source of his supernatural strength, given to him by me, the Lord his God, to help fight his enemies, the Philistines. Your hair is the supernatural strength I have given you to help you fight your enemies, America! Your hair, *my child*, is the source of your supernatural strength to help you overcome all the adversity that has come into your life, whether you asked for it, or not!"

"So how can my hair be used of God as a supernatural weapon of strength in my life?"

God specifically tells you, *"And even the very hairs of your head are all numbered."* (Matthew 10:30, Luke 12:7)

"As a nation, I can tell you the exact number of hairs on all your heads," says the Lord. "I told *my people* that, and then afterwards I told them not to be afraid of those who can kill the body."

"Do not be afraid of those who kill the body, but cannot kill the soul. Rather, be afraid of the One who can destroy both soul and body in hell." (Matthew 10:28, Luke 12:4)

"I said this to tell you that violent acts of crime and terrorism can kill people as you have seen in recent days, but they cannot kill souls. If you were to ask me to tell you the very number of hairs on your head, I would give you a very specific number," says the Lord.

"What if I'm bald?"

"I would say to you, your head pertains to any part of your body that is above your neck, you warped-minded spirit. That includes your nose, your ears, your eyebrows, your mustache, and even your beard. So the very hairs of your head are all numbered, even if you're bald!"

"What about a cancer patient you won't heal, or didn't heal?"

"I, the Lord your God, would say to you, they have no hair because of the treatments they are receiving, in fighting the cancerous disease. Just as you have no common sense in you, because of the treatments Satan has given your mind over your ruined life, trying to blind you of what little faith you have in me," says the Lord!

"Cancer isn't from me, you snake! Just like murder, and other acts of violent crime that lead to death, aren't of me either. Just like the corruption of lies, greed and perversion within your own government aren't of me," says the Lord. "That is why it has been eating away at the morality in your society, exactly like cancer eats away at the body of a person. It comes from the pit of hell itself, right along with your warped-minded attitudes toward me, the Lord your God, over what you call unanswered prayers."

"Has anyone ever told you?

'For my thoughts are not your thoughts, neither are your ways my ways, declares the Lord! As the heavens are higher than the earth, so are my ways higher than your ways and my thoughts than your thoughts.'
(Isaiah 55:8-9)

"Those who are no longer with you because of cancer, or violent acts of crime, had their days numbered in this life like you do. Just as I have the very hairs of your head all numbered, so I can even tell you the very number of days of life you have left to live if I chose to. But I won't!"

"Are you kidding?"

"You would then take it upon yourself to do as you please, just like you already do, up until the last day of this earthly life you live. Then, on the day before your last day, you would totally and whole heartedly give your life to me, while fasting and praying your way through a barrage of forgiveness pleas over everything you did that you weren't supposed to do. You would weep and cry before me, in an effort to move me into letting you into my Kingdom of eternal life. But because of your stubborn, selfish, self-centered heart, you would not enter.

"But I will reply, 'I never knew you. Get away from me, you who break God's laws.'" (Matthew 7:23 NLT)

"But Lord, you just said, 'Before you formed me in the womb, you knew me!'"

"That's my point! Don't play games with me, because I do know you, even before you were ever born. Give me a chance to really come alive in you, *my child*! Stop playing church with me," says the Lord. "Stop playing mind games with me! I AM the Lord your God, and there is no other! You people come at me with the same attitudes with which the

Pharisees and the teachers of the law came at me. You are always questioning and contradicting everything I AM trying to teach you, *my people*, in this dying and uncaring world in which you live. As a nation, you are taught religion, and church rituals and doctrines, instead of my true living word. I will tell you who do this very thing, the same that I told them amongst whom I walked,

"Woe to you, teachers of the law and Pharisees, you hypocrites! You shut the door of the kingdom of heaven in people's faces. You yourselves do not enter, nor will you let those enter who are trying to."
(Matthew 23:13)

"That is exactly what you are trying to do, because of your anger issues towards me, the Lord your God. Keep reading what is prophetically being written for you to read, if you want a divine intervention and change in your life," says the Lord. "If not, don't waste your selfish time on me," says the Lord. "It won't change me, or ruin me as it has you, *my child*. It won't ruin, or affect my kingdom the way it has ruined your nation."

"Heaven and earth will pass away; but my words will never pass away."
(Luke 21:33)

"I AM the Lord, and I do not change. That is why you descendants of Jacob, are not already destroyed."   (Malachi 3:6 NLT)

"From this day forward, your life will never be the same again for you," says the Lord. "America will never be the same again!"

"So is my word that goes out from my mouth; <u>IT WILL NOT</u> return to me empty, <u>BUT WILL ACCOMPLISH</u> what I desire and achieve the purpose for which I sent it."   (Isaiah 55:11)

"Keep this book of the law always on your lips. <u>MEDITATE</u> on it day and night, so that you may be careful to do everything written in it. <u>THEN</u> you will be prosperous and successful. Have I not commanded you? Be strong and courageous! Do not be afraid; do not be

discouraged, for the Lord your God will be with you wherever you go."
(Joshua 1:8-9)

"I AM here this day to make you strong and courageous," says the Lord. "Do you know what the problem is with the majority of you, *my people,* whether you live for me, or not? You always have to find someone, or something, to blame for your dilemmas in the lives you live. Someone broke your heart! Someone violated you! Someone lost your trust, someone cheated on you, someone lied about you while gossiping about you. Someone did *whatever* to you!"

"Then there's the issues of life, the worries of life and the deceitfulness of wealth; bills, loss of jobs, credit card fraud and hackers who steal identities and money and lying con artists everywhere!"

"Then there's me, God, the one who didn't heal a loved one who passed away; the one who allowed an evil act of crime that took a loved one from you, even though I hate and resent evil acts of behavior. I AM the one who allowed nature - the weather - to take everything, all you worked your entire life for, in a few hours…Thanks to God! That's about the only 'thanks' I get from *my people*, when disaster strikes, or you get a broken heart over the loss of a loved one. Other than that, I only exist in the heavens of the invisible world."

"In fact, I was, and have been in existence, way before you were ever thought of, long before you came into existence. I told you in my word, 'In this world you live in, you would have trouble. But take heart! I have overcome the world (John 16:33).' However, how can you take anything to heart of me, the Lord your God! You don't even take time to accept me into your life and know me as your personal Lord and Savior!"

"I told you at the very start of this conversation: I chose you before the creation of the world. America, I destined you <u>BEFORE</u> the foundations of the world were even laid. I did the same for you, *my child*, as I did Samson, my chosen one."

"Where you people of mine go wrong is this: you treat my word like you do a restaurant. It has a menu with words written on it from all sorts of food to choose from. Don't want it or like it, don't order it? Don't eat it! Like it and want it, then order it, and eat it! After all, you are the one who is going to pay for it."

"That's exactly true of my word, too. You read a word of prosperity, or healing; you accept it whole heartedly, and believe it. You take hold of it with all the inner strength and faith you can muster up in your efforts of obtaining whatever it is you are after."

"Then, you read a passage of my word that says, 'Love your enemies. Forgive those who hurt you. Pray for those who mistreat you.' You cringe from within, and with all the strength you can muster up, you resist my word and totally ignore it, since it doesn't appeal to you. After all, you are the one who is going to pay for it, no matter what you choose."

"My point is, if you are going to stand on my word as an act of faith towards me, the Lord your God, for me to help you with your life, and your nation - then take it in its whole context. Not in portions to satisfy your own evil appetite."

"Selfishness only seeks itself, and no one else. That includes me, the Lord your God! What do you tell this generation of children, the youth, about what has happened to them in this degrading, immoral society? What do you tell them about their example, those whom you raise to believe in me?"

"They are the victims of divorce, sexual assaults, and perversion. They live in broken homes that involve all types of abuse, leaving them confused, wondering why there are no real fathers or mothers in their lives. Why are mom and dad the same sex living together as one? Two men or two women living together! Who are their real parents?"

"Are we judging now? Don't worry! There are plenty of homes that have a man and woman living in them as mom and dad, who are too busy with their own lives, through work, or social media. If they tend to their children like they do their cell phones, televisions or computers, or even their jobs, then those children might acknowledge they do have parents."

"Maybe if they spent more time with their children, as much as they do drinking, drugs and partying, shopping for personal appearance items to look good, yet are worth nothing, then things might be different. Your children see all your bed partners that come and go into your insecure lives. I can't blame a child for his or her behavior, because of the parents' behavior, and lifestyles."

"What about the Mom and Dad who did raise and train their children in the way they should go, but the child simply didn't. Who is to blame there? The parents? Too much God and Jesus Christ? Too much church? Too many strict guidelines? Someone else is always to blame."

"Whether you had it good or bad in your life, the choices you made, or will make in your life are *on you* as an individual, and even as a nation. In fact, the very hairs on your head are all still numbered of me," says the Lord. "There isn't an issue in your life I know nothing about."

"You must go back to your child-like faith, the faith that you had in your life at one time, in order for me to help you," says the Lord. "You can start with the truth I just gave you... I know the <u>EXACT</u> number of hairs on your head; the very secret to Samson's supernatural strength he possessed in his life."

"So, if I know that much about you, then there cannot be anything that I don't know about you. I know things that you don't even know about yourself. I know of every dark, deep, hidden secret of regret you are carrying around as a burden to your soul that no one knows anything about. I know the thing that is just eating away at you inwardly, eating you alive within your soul and your spirit."

"There is nothing concealed that will not be disclosed, or hidden that will not be made known."   *(Luke 12:2)*

"No matter how dark and dismal it looks, or how hopeless it has gotten for you, I know you still believe in me, the Lord your God, even as a nation!"

"The Lord said, 'I have indeed seen the misery of my people in Egypt (America). *I have heard their crying out because of their slave drivers* (corrupted government, churches, faiths, denominations and religions) *and* I AM *concerned about their suffering.'"* (Exodus 3:7)

"You are *my people* I speak of!" says the Lord. "I have seen your misery, and I have heard your cries. I AM concerned about your suffering. I haven't lost count of the very hairs on your head, and I <u>NEVER</u> will," says the Lord. "No matter how far you feel I AM from you, or how dark it seems all around you, My eyes, and My light, can pierce the greatest darkness the kingdom of hell can put between you and Me," says the Lord. "As far as the distance you feel between us, there is no distance that exists where my loving arms cannot reach you, *My child*. There is no distance between you and Me, America!"

"This was to fulfill the word of Isaiah the prophet: 'Lord, who has believed our message and to whom has the arm of the Lord been revealed?' For this reason they could not believe, because, as Isaiah says elsewhere, 'He has blinded their eyes and deadened their hearts, so they can neither see with their eyes, nor understand with their hearts, nor turn – **and I WOULD HEAL THEM.***'"* (John 12:38-40)

"That is why I AM begging you to give me just a little bit of your undivided attention, so you can stay focused with your eyes on Me, and listen with your ears in what you are being told this very day and hour about your life," says the Lord. "That is why."

"Isaiah said this because he saw Jesus' glory and spoke about him."
(John 12:41)

CHAPTER THREE

Samson's Gift

"Samson went down to Timnah together with his father and his mother. As they approached the vineyards, suddenly a young lion came roaring towards him. The Spirit of the Lord came powerfully upon him so that he tore the lion apart with his bare hands as he might have torn a young goat. But he told neither his father nor his mother what he had done." (Judges 14:5-6)

"Then three thousand men from Judah went down to the cave in the rock of Etam and said to Samson; don't you realize that the Philistines are rulers over us? What have you done to us? He answered; I merely did to them what they did to me! They said to him; we've come to tie you up and hand you over to the Philistines. Samson said; swear to me that you won't kill me yourselves." Agreed they answered; we will only tie you up and hand you over to them. We will not kill you. So they bound him with two new ropes and lead him up from the rock. As he approached Lehi, the Philistines came towards him shouting. "The Spirit of the Lord" came powerfully upon him. The ropes on his arms became like charred flax and the bindings dropped from his hands. Finding a fresh jawbone of a donkey, he grabbed it and struck down a thousand men."
(Judges 15:11-15)

"One day Samson went to Gaza where he saw a prostitute. He went in to

spend the night with her. The people of Gaza were told; Samson is here! So they surrounded the place and lay in wait for him all night at the city gate. They made no move during the night; saying: At dawn we will kill him. But Samson lay there only until the middle of the night. Then he got up and took hold of the doors of the city gate together with the two posts and tore them loose bar and all. He lifted them to his shoulders and carried them to the top of the hill that faces Hebron."   *(Judges 16:1-3)*

"Talk about a super hero! One who can fight off any enemy, or enemy strategy, that comes against him. You people seem to be fascinated by fictional characters and super heroes. You literally spend millions and millions of dollars to see super heroes in your movie theaters and on your television screens. You even buy super hero books, novels, movies and comic books by the millions," says God.

"My Samson was no fictional character! He was as non-fictional as they come. His existence in this life was as real as your own life is now, as real as this lifetime you are now living. He possessed his supernatural strength through his obedience to me in whatever he did."

"What? Wait a minute! I just read that he went and laid with a prostitute ... and he still had his strength through the power of your Spirit?"

"Yes, he did! I told you earlier, there's not one righteous among you. That goes to show that you still don't have your mind totally set on my Son, Christ Jesus, as you were told to do at the beginning of this message. You are totally focused on being perfect towards me before I can help you in your life. So, I guess my Son's death on the cross was a consolation prize to you, just in case you can't reach perfection in your-own efforts of living a sinless life! I wish you would read my word more often than you do. You would know the very reason why my Son Jesus Christ appeared in this earth of yours in the first place."

"The one who does what is sinful is of the devil, because the devil has been sinning from the beginning. The reason the Son of God appeared was to destroy the devil's work."   *(1 John 3:8)*
"In Samson's time, my Son hadn't yet appeared! They had their own

sacrifices for their sins towards me, the Lord their God. But you want it all to make sense to you before you can believe that I, the Lord your God, truly love you with all my heart."

"Get real with me, *my child*! Get real with me, America! If you would read my word, you would know you reap what you sow!"

"Really? I see people doing all sorts of evil while prospering, while those who try to do the right things suffer greatly."

"So you convince yourself, I AM an unjust God! Then live to your preference as you do desire. But it is written for you,

"God is not unjust; he will never forget your work and the love you have shown him as you have helped his people and continue to help them."
(Hebrews 6:10)

"Maybe by the end of this message, I can convince you, whole heartedly, that I truly love you more than you would have ever imagined. But just by obeying the command his mother got from the angelic visitation before his birth, and what his parents told him (Samson) about his hair was the reason for his supernatural strength. Not a single strand of your hair will fall to the ground from your head without my knowledge," says the Lord!

"You are a super power America! What's happened to you? You are my son! You are my daughter! Where are you, my chosen one? This generation of youth are taking out their own parents! Yet, the same parents are taking out their babies and children too! Children are taking out children."

"Why? We are dealing with the spirit of the Philistines. This spirit wants nothing less than to take out the youth of this nation…in fact, this same evil spirit wants to completely destroy and take you out as a nation!"

"So, you can lay down all the excuses you can come up with to explain why things are the way they are. Lay them down, before they side track you in what I AM trying to get across to you in this message. Even if what you say is true, about all that has happened, STOP IT! Your life is not controlled by what has happened to it. Your country isn't controlled by what has happened to it, either."

"Yes it is, Lord! Because you allowed it!"

"Can you lay down everything, and everyone, just for a little while? Let's act as though you and I, the Lord your God, are all that exist on this earth, and nothing else. It's easy to do! You have done it all your life, except in an opposite form, or mode. Before today, everything, and everyone, existed in your life except me, the Lord your God! So now let's do it in reverse!"

"No one else exists now, at this very moment, except you and me, the Lord your God, God of heaven, who created you in his image."

"Say you are one who never had parents, and if you did, it was a single parent home. Or, you grew up in a house with your dad, but the woman he was with wasn't your mother, or vice versa, the man your mother married isn't your father. Maybe your life wouldn't have turned out the mess it did."

"Really? I've seen homes where stepfathers and stepmothers were the best thing that happened to that child who didn't have their real father, or their real mother because of divorce situations."

"But even worse than that," says God, "I have seen the homes who had the real father, and real mother, be there for their child from the day of their birth, all the way up to - and through - the days of hardship, and total rebellion. It still turned out to be a disastrous life for that child. Needless to say, it was disastrous for the parents too, who got put through a ringer doing everything they could to help their child; yet, to no avail."

"Let's say you did have the greatest father and mother to walk the face of the earth. Your life went great, a total success story, with hardly any failures about which to complain. Then, all of a sudden, mom and dad die in a violent act of crime of murder against them, or were taken out by a drunk driver."

"What then? Are you going to blame me, God, for losing your parents? You may as well. Everybody else does! I can't even be thanked for giving someone a mother, or a father, to cherish all the days of his life. It's even one of the commandments written!"

"Honor your father and mother"- which is the first commandment with a promise." *(Ephesians 6:2)*

"It's hard to honor a father, or a mother, who had nothing to do with you, one who was never in your life. How about those who were violated by their parents? Should you honor them?"

"The phrase, "to honor them", means that you are telling me, God, "Thank you for using them to bring me into existence, so I can be used of you, Lord, in any way you would want to use me."

"But no! You want to obtain your love, security, and your inner peace from your father and mother on earth."

"The reason you honor your father and mother, is so you can get your promise from me: **your gift**! But, so long as you keep putting mom and dad issues first in your life before me, the Lord your God, you will never get your gift of strength. This is the same gift Samson had in his life, to overcome all the adversity of his enemies - his supernatural strength!"

"I guess no one has ever told you that you were literally given a gift of strength from me, the Lord your God. My Son Jesus Christ told you about the gift he was going to give you. Upon giving you that gift, you would receive supernatural strength in this life to overcome all the adversity which the devil would throw at you."

"Jesus told all of you, *"If you love me, obey my commands. I will ask the Father, and he will give you another friend to help you and to be with*

you forever. That friend is the Spirit of Truth. The world can't accept him. That's because the world does not see him or know him. But you know him. He lives with you, and he will be in you. I will not leave you like children who don't have parents. I will come to you."
(John 14:15-18 NIRV)

"The promise is for you and your children and for all who are far off – for all whom the Lord our God will call."   *(Acts 2:39)*

"My promise to you is through my Holy Spirit, whom you will see by the time you finish this message. My Spirit is the part of me that longs to be loved by all *my people*. But because of so much hardship this world, satan's kingdom, lashes out at *my child*ren with, millions have a hard time staying focused on their faith in me, the Lord your God."

"You will see my gift of love displayed for you at the end of this message to you. I promise you! But, first, I must convince you that I know exactly what you are going through, and dealing with, right at this very hour in your own life."

"In the prime of his life, Samson made it known to the world that I was his God, by the actions of his faith and obedience in his life, just as you did at one time in your life as my son, my daughter, and even my country, America. As a nation, you boldly inscribed it on all your currency, "In God We Trust"! And I know you still do. I will never fail you, America! I will never fail you, my son, or you, my daughter!"

"Why is it that everybody had it in for Samson? It is for the same reason everybody has it in for you as an individual, or even as a nation: *"If the world hates you, keep in mind that it hated me first. If you belonged to the world, it would* love *you as its own. As it is, you do not belong to the world, but I have chosen you out of the world. That is why the world hates you."*   *(John 15:18-19)*

"You are more than a conqueror in Christ Jesus!"

"Can anything ever separate us from Christ's Love? Does it mean he no

longer loves us if we have trouble or calamity, or are persecuted, or hungry, or destitute, or in danger, or threatened with death? (As the scriptures say, "for your sake we are killed every day; we are being slaughtered like sheep) No! Despite all these things, <u>OVERWHELMING</u> victory is ours through Christ who loved us. And I AM convinced that <u>NOTHING</u> can ever separate us from God's Love. Neither death nor life, neither angels nor demons, neither our fears for today nor our worries about tomorrow- not even the powers of hell can separate us from God's Love. No power in the sky above or on the earth below- indeed, nothing in all creation will ever be able to separate us from the Love of God <u>that is revealed in Christ Jesus our Lord."</u> (Romans 8:35-39 NLT)

"So, now you need to realize, and accept, that you are more than a conqueror in Christ Jesus, my Son, and **_NOT YOURSELF!_** Right? I want that to sink into your head, brain, and mind, so you can overcome all the adversity that has come into your life, and against your nation."

"The reason this is important is: Nothing you have done, or are even doing now as I speak to you, will separate my Love from you, *my child*, America! NOTHING! I will love you until the day you die, says the Lord! The <u>ONLY</u> separation that exists between you and me, the Lord your God, is you saying, "No" to my Son in your life before you die, or before I call you home into my presence."

"There is a judge for the one who rejects me and does not accept my words, the very words I have spoken will condemn him at the last day."
(John 12:48)

"That is why I said, 'You are more than a conqueror in Christ Jesus,' my Son, and not in yourself! That is satan's first priority in your life, and in your nation of America - to separate you from me, the Lord your God, and Jesus Christ, for all eternity."

"*My people* don't have a problem with faith. Why? Because,

"Faith is the substance of things hoped for, the evidence of things not seen." (Hebrews 11:1 KJV)

"The biggest problem with the majority of you is **obedience**! You want a simple example of obedience? Let's use this perverse generation as an example. It doesn't take much faith to become a mom, or a dad, does it? Just get together with another person, opposite the sex gender you are, of course! Same sex couples can't produce children. Then through your lust and perversion you will conceive between the two of you."

"The faith used by the male gender was to satisfy his lust passion he had on him, while the female gender had the same drive on her, with the intentions of hopefully finding someone to love her as his own. Then the child comes, making the both of you the parents - mom and dad!"

"Faith mission accomplished. Now be a real father, and a real mother to that child according to my word, even though you totally skipped the part about the two becoming one, before conceiving children."

"That's not hard, God! I AM the child's father, and she's the child's mother, married or not! What's your point?"

"If you did it **my way**, according to my written word, it literally changes everything in, and around, your personal lives, making you become responsible adults to the children. It would change this nation's morality level, and attitude of aborting children before they are born. It would change the attitude of marriage created of me, the Lord your God, intended to be between a man and a woman."

"Be a real father and husband! Be a real mother and wife! Got me? Of course you do!"

"Are you kidding, Lord? We are still the child's father and mother whether we get married, or not."

"You stubborn people! You are heathen at heart and deaf to the truth. Must you forever resist the "Holy Spirit"? That's what your ancestors did, and so do you!" *(Acts 7:51 NLT)*

"Then why was your unborn child aborted? Why do you give your children up for adoption? That's what some of you reading these words are trying to figure out, "Why wasn't I wanted by my mom, or my dad?"

"Why are you angry about child support you have to pay, and you don't even get to see your child? And you, young lady, why do you use your child support on yourself, and not your child's needs?"

"And what kind of moms and dads are you, entertaining all types of men and women whom you're not married to, in your bed, right in front of your children to see?"

"I try and talk common sense to you, and you still come at me with warped-minded attitudes. That is what changed the course of Samson's life. Samson fell in love! That was the beginning of his woes."

"Lord, are you condemning love?"

"No! What happens is that when one encounters love for another person, I, the Lord your God, become a very distant second in your life. I AM not only speaking of human affection for one another. It also pertains to other things in your life that make me, God, less important, and almost non-existent in your life."

"As human beings, you know that feeling. As a child growing up, mom and dad's self-interest and passions became first priority to them in their very busy lives, making you feel non-existent; yet, the whole time you felt that way, I was with you before you were ever born."

"But, then, you have moms and dads who totally give their whole lives away for the sake of their children. Of course some want their children to be successful, famous, and financially stable by their efforts of putting it all out there for them. You would be surprised how many children don't really care, or even have an interest in what you so desire for them. So you have them imprisoned within their own beings, through fear of telling you the truth of what they really want in their lives you so desperately want to try and control."

"Then I have the moms and dads who are constantly, tearfully crying to me, 'Lord, where did I go wrong with *my child*ren?'"

"My answer would be: you deliberately disobeyed my word in raising and training your children in the way they should go."

"What word?"

"Anyone who loves their father or mother more than me is not worthy of me; anyone who loves theirs son or daughter more than me is not worthy of me." *(Matthew 10:37)*

"It doesn't mean you won't be with me in eternity because you love your family members so much. It simply means you don't deserve my spirit of love and peace in your own personal life, since you are relying on obtaining it from your loved ones, instead of from me, the Lord your God! You worship your loved ones lives more than you do mine. That's if I even exist in your life!"

"I know I AM speaking of family here, but this pertains to life in general, too! You are so unhappy within yourselves. What you thought would bring you happiness has only brought you misery, and despair. You do just what parents have done for their children: You gave them everything they ever wanted, and said they needed, even if it broke you, and you totally went against your own beliefs and values, only to be forgotten; then you are treated in the end as though you never really existed."

"I know that feeling firsthand," says the Lord, your God. "The time will come in your life that you will begin to want to feel that you belong to something, or someone. You will soul search for companionship, when the whole time you have had it with me, the Lord your God, whom you have totally ignored."

"I know it's hard to comprehend, because I AM an invisible being that exists in a world that goes by what is visible to them. Man must see before he believes! I even told the people that same thing when I walked the face of the earth."

"Unless you people see signs and wonders," Jesus told him, "you will never believe." *(John 4:48)*

"That is why distractions are the very core of blindness *my people* have towards me, the Lord their God. Even if what you search for is good for you, such as a spouse, a house with a mortgage, a career, education, friends, jobs, and so on, I become secondary in everyone's life, regardless. When Samson met Delilah and fell in love, that's when his test of faith and obedience came into play. Once Satan sees you get distracted, he veers you off course from our relationship. He will use whoever, or whatever it is in your life, that has become part of your life, if not your life itself."

"So, what Lord? Don't go after anything in this life, really?"

"I AM the one who said:

"The thief comes only to steal and kill and destroy; I have come that they may have life, and have it to the full." *(John 10:10)*

"In other words, I want you to succeed in this life you live. Just don't abandon me for anything, or anyone, in your life, even if it turns out to be a success. Because then your success will be first priority in your life, that when I demand your life from you, where will your faith be - in me, or your success?"

"That's why I asked you:

"What good is it for someone to gain the whole world; yet forfeit their soul?" *(Matthew 16:26, Mark 8:36)*

"And who will get everything, and everyone, you leave behind, while you go into outer darkness, where there will be weeping and gnashing of teeth for having me as second priority in your life?"

"Now, since I have become second to everyone's goals and dreams in their personal lives, and even in this nation, the evil spirits rule over every one of you, and over this nation as a whole."

"That's what happened to Samson, my chosen one! All his brute, supernatural strength was no match for the spiritual encounter he was about to face. I was still with Samson when he fell in love with Delilah, just as I AM with you. I won't abandon you because of love and success; in fact, I won't abandon you for anyone, or anything in this life," says the Lord. "Just stop putting me second in your life!"

"Why? Everybody wanted to know the secret of Samson's strength. Guess who they went to? Satan used it to reveal the secret of his strength, that would lead him to his greatest weakness. They went to the woman Samson fell in love with, the love of his life! The super heroism of Samson was about to meet its match."

"The rulers of the Philistines went to Delilah to see if they could lure Samson into revealing the secret to his strength. The Delilah spirit came three times to Samson, asking him to reveal the secret to his super natural strength. Three times Samson revealed a strategy to her that would subdue him. Three times Delilah acted on his words, only to be fooled over again."

"How many times have people showed their envy towards you personally, or even as a nation, because of your faith in me, the Lord your God? How many times have they questioned it? How many times have they challenged it? How many times has Satan put you with your back against the wall, using those you love as your own to doubt my existence in your life," says the Lord.

"How many times did you overcome satan in his quest through your faith in the Lord your God?"

"Why did you overcome? Because you kept your faith in the Lord your God that you serve, and believe in, my daughter, my son, AMERICA! The one who has all of the very hairs numbered on your head."

CHAPTER FOUR

Samson's Test

"There comes a point in time in your life that I, the Lord your God, will allow the enemy to take you off course by your own temptations through the lust of the flesh. Why? For one,

"When tempted, no one should say, "God is tempting me". For God cannot be tempted by evil, nor does he tempt anyone; but each person is tempted when they are dragged away by their own evil desire and enticed. Then, after desire has conceived, it gives birth to sin; and sin, when it is full-grown, gives birth to death." Don't be deceived, my dear brothers and sisters." *(James 1:13-16)*

"Secondly, temptation from sin enables one to grow in me, the Lord your God, if they choose to, only to prove to satan, the enemy of your soul, your loyalty to your God in heaven you worship and serve."

"Blessed is the one who perseveres under trial because, having stood the test, that person will receive the crown of life that the Lord has promised to those who love him." *(James 1:12)*

"I want you to understand what it is to love me, the Lord your God! It is total commitment to our relationship! I want you to notice I said, 'your commitment to our relationship,' right? Not 'commitment to being like me'! If I held you to my standard, and character of being Holy, like me, no one in all of humanity would make it into heaven with me."

"What's my relationship to you? You either love me, or you don't! Most of you do love me, or you wouldn't be crying out to me from within your souls, feeling unworthy of me," says the Lord. "Just because it seems as though no one cares about you, and your life doesn't mean a thing to anyone around you, I AM not the same as those in, and around, your life."

"I have always loved you, even before you were born. I held you in my arms before putting you on this earth. I still long to hold you in my arms, *my child*! I long to hold you in my arms, America! Yet you resist me, thinking I AM like everyone else is around you in your life. As I said before, you will see my love for you when we finish this message. You will witness my help for you, just as I helped Samson in his life."

"Some time later, he fell in love with a woman in the valley of Sorek whose name was Delilah. The rulers of the Philistines went to her and said, See if you can lure him into showing you the secret of his great strength and how we can overpower him so we may tie him up and subdue him. Each one of us will give you eleven hundred shekels of silver. So Delilah said to Samson; tell me the secret of your great strength and how you can be tied up and subdued. Samson answered her; if anyone ties me with seven fresh bow strings that had not been dried, I'll become as weak as any other man. Then the rulers of the Philistines brought her seven fresh bowstrings that had not been dried and she tied him up with them. With men hidden in the room, she called to him, Samson, the Philistines are upon you. But he snapped the bowstring as easily as a piece of string snaps when it comes close to a flame. So the secret of his strength wasn't discovered. Then Delilah said to Samson, "You have made a fool of me, you lied to me. Come now, tell me how you can be tied. He said, If anyone ties me securely with new ropes that have never been used; I'll be as weak as any other man. So Delilah took new ropes and tied him with them. Then with men hidden in the room, she called to him; Samson the Philistines are upon you! But he snapped the ropes off his arms as if they were threads. Delilah then said

to Samson; "All this time you gave been making a fool of me lying to me. Tell me now how you can be tied. He replied, "If you weave the seven braids of my head into the fabric on the loom and tighten it with a pin; I'll become as weak as any other man." So while he was sleeping, Delilah took the seven braids of his head, wove them into the fabric and tightened it with a pin. Again she called to him, Samson, the Philistines are upon you! He awoke from his sleep and pulled the pin and the loom with the fabric."   *(Judges 16:4-14)*

"Temptation, and being tempted, is an element that shows its face to every human being on the face of the earth. Believe it or not, I faced it too," says the Lord. "I had just finished a forty day fast in the desert when the tempter came to test me. But every temptation he came at me with, I responded: 'It is written! It is written!'"

"Heaven's word rules over the earth, when taken in its full context. Remember I told you how people treat my word like they do a restaurant? I overcame satan through the written word. When it came to one of my own chosen twelve, money was the driving force to my betrayal. Thirty silver pieces to be exact!"

"Now the feast of the unleavened bread, called the Passover, was approaching and the chief priests and the teachers of the law were looking for some way to get rid of Jesus, for they were afraid of the people. Then Satan *entered Judas, called Iscariot, one of the twelve. And Judas went to the chief priests and officers of the temple guard and discussed with them how he might betray Jesus. They were delighted and agreed to give him money."*   *(Matthew 26:14-16, Luke 22:1-5)*

"That's exactly what Delilah did to Samson - all for silver! You very well know, and have seen with your own eyes, that people in your society you live with will do crazy, out of this world things against you when it comes to money (silver) being involved."

"Of all places, you see it in your corrupted government, with oil price gouging, lavish spending of your hard earned tax dollars on personal vacation travels, and personal use. But then there are those of you who freeload off your government incentives, since you don't care to work; while those who do work, work their fingers to the bone supporting your lazy gluttony!"

"Oh! How can I forget the greed that surfaces when one passes away. Total greed! You never had any part in the deceased's life, but now you are first in line to collect personal belongings and finances of the deceased!"

"You'd be amazed at how many there are who betray their faith over money, preaching a gospel of prosperity, while souls pass on to the next life, never accepting me into their own life. How many times have you been used for money? Practically the whole world revolves around money. Money has locked up millions in prison, behind bars over drug selling and distributing. Tax evasions! Child support! Acts of fraud! Printing counterfeit currency! You get my point? Right?"

"Not only did Delilah accept the bribe of silver shekels, but she wanted to be the one to take Samson down, to prove to herself and everyone else the power she had in her life. What she did was similar to what an abuser does to his or her victim, and like spouses do to their mates! They love the feeling of having power and control over your life, your soul, and your spirit."

"That is what you are up against, every day of your life. Delilah spirits (people) who want to help the Philistines (satan's spirits) take you down, in order for you to see who rules your life, heart and soul. Peer pressure, or as it's called in a young child's life, bullying!"

"Once satan sets his mind on totally destroying you and your faith, he will use whatever, and whoever, is closest to you in your life, since it's not me, the Lord your God! He will use your wife, your husband, your children, your family, your friends (if you want to call them that), your job, your finances, your evil memories of your childhood life that no one knows anything about. He especially likes to use mistakes you have made that you can't seem to forgive yourself of, or even forget."

"In Samson's time, the Philistines represented Israel's enemies. Israel represents *my people*! So in this very time frame in your life, you are my Israel, and the Philistines are the enemies of your soul at work in your life I created in my image. Satan has only one desire for your life: Death! This death isn't when you physically die, but when you die and never make it into heaven because you gave up on your faith in me, the Lord your God!"

"The time of testing in your life is triggered by the voices that taunt you in your head over your failures in your life; or, they intimidate you, saying, 'You will never amount to anything! You're a total failure! You should never have been born! Pretty bad, your mother or father never wanted you.'"

"Those are invisible voices that talk to you when you're alone, soul searching for answers to your heartache and sorrows. Not to mention your regrets! Even if one can't hear in the physical realm, they hear in the invisible realm."

"Then you have the physical voices, who are no more than people who can't stand you, or are jealous of you. They lie, gossip, slander, make false accusations, and spread all types of rumors about others, rumors that have no truth to them. I know millions of those who claim to be followers of mine, yet they destroy others through their mouths that speak lies from hell."

"Hell?"

"Yes, hell! If they were from me, the Lord your God, they would build a person up, not tear them down. That is why I AM here with you today at this very moment -- to build you up, and to tear down all the walls of the enemy that have you imprisoned to your own fears and doubts."

"It's not always gossip that tears people's lives apart! Just simple peer pressure will do it. People saying to you, 'Come on man! Try this once! It'll get your mind off everything and everyone. Your wife will never find out, your husband will never find out. Just do it once; and if you don't care for it, that's alright; at least you tried!'"

"These voices are then joined by those invisible voices on a more powerful level of coming at you, saying, 'Ah! Just kill yourself man! Nobody cares about you anyway. You fought for your country, and you even lost buddies over there in the time of combat, because you didn't do enough. You could've done more! But you didn't even try! You even killed people, and civilians, who were innocent. Especially taking out a child before it was even born! Murderer! What purpose do you serve in this life?' These Voices are from the dungeons of hell, taunting your mind, and crucifying you over past mistakes."

"How about you, who are so conscious about your looks? You look at yourself in the mirror who-knows-how-many-times-a-day, weeks, or even years while listening to voices telling you, 'You're fat! You're Overweight! You're unattractive! You will never be attractive! That's why mom and dad got divorced and left you. It's your fault! You were a mistake! No guy or girl will ever want you because of your looks. Wait till they find out about your dark secrets of sexual abuse you endured from one you never expected it. That's why you get picked on so much! Kill yourself! No one will even notice you are gone!"

"Of all things, the Voices love to tell you, 'God doesn't even care about you! He's supposed to be God, and all he does is just sit on his throne in heaven watching you suffer, without any intervention of any kind. And you call that hope? Having faith in someone who doesn't even care! What kind of God is that?'"

"These Voices come straight from the pit of hell, insulting and mocking the God of heaven and earth, who created you in His image. These are the same spirits from hell that have tormented you, and tortured you for years without end, and no one has even noticed, especially in this young generation."

"The youth who are pushed by their parents' dreams and desires for their children, instead of the child being themselves and choosing what, and who, they want to be. They are playing sports while entertaining everyone around, yet being miserable and in hell, trying to not disappoint those around you. Attending College to only make yourself try to be somebody you're not!"

"Is this really a message from God? It sounds very wicked, and evil, and so discouraging!"

"Discouraging? No! I AM calling out the spirits as they are in the midst of *my people,*" says the Lord. "My slave-driven youth that, over the centuries, is only getting worse as time goes by since no one teaches them of me," says the Lord. "You just teach them **about** me, not of me! There is a HUGE difference in what you teach of one, and how you teach it."

"I can tell you a lot about a person you don't even know, and even point him out to you. Once I do, you then see him again without me being present, and you will know him by what you were told about him by me. But if you went to him yourself, and got to know him better, you might find that I lied about him, or not told you everything about him that he has told you of himself. That is my burning desire within my Spirit," says the Lord.

"This is what the Lord says to Israel: Seek me and live!"   *(Amos 5:4)*

"I'm talking to you, *my people*, too! When you give in to others' actions and wishes, just to fit in, you only harm yourself more than those around you. When Delilah nagged Samson, she continued persistently to nag, and nag, and nag Samson, making him grow weary and tired to the point of exhaustion. Sort of like people do to you who go to the gym to stay strong, and in shape; yet you grow weak in the time of nagging, and crying, from a crybaby who doesn't get their way."

"Delilah continued to nag Samson, pushing him to reveal his secret of his supernatural strength, before falling asleep in her arms and lap. She said, 'I thought you loved me, but all you have done is made a fool of me.'"

"You parents tell your children that, when they fail you in fulfilling your vision you wanted for them, which is your eyes' and heart's desire. You children tell your parents that, when they won't support your choice of lifestyle in comparison to how you were raised. You boys tell girls that all the time, when they won't sexually give in to your lustful desires, 'I really thought you loved me! ' Then when they do give in to you, a few months later you get hit with child support, and you cry unto them again saying, 'Why are you doing this to me? I thought you loved me, and you wanted a baby!'"

"You girls are so easily persuaded by a teared-up boy in your arms, begging for your body, while the whole time you're convinced they truly love you, and it's your sexuality they're after. My Son Jesus cries every day over you, because he loves you, and you don't even give it a thought, not even for one second, to hold him in your arms. He wants your heart like no one else ever will."

"That goes for all of you men and women who served your country. You literally gave your lives in the trenches of combat, and war, fighting the evil in this world. You wholeheartedly gave it all you had, from within your heart and soul for this country you are so proud of. You survived a war zone with your life being spared, only to come home and fight a greater war within your own mind, one that torments you night and day. Yet no one even notices, or even seems to care."

"You cry and rage from within your own soul and being, 'Damn this country and its government, and the people too! I thought all of you really loved me for protecting and serving this country.' You were totally focused on everything, and everyone, around you, trying to find your inner peace and contentment from people, in general, who would acknowledge your service. Yet you never looked my way," says the Lord. "I honor you in my heart, and I love you like no one ever has, or ever will. If there is anyone who understands you and your heart-felt broken heartedness, it would be me, the Lord your God, laying down my life for my friends!"

"Greater love has no one than this: to lay down one's life for one's friends." *(John 15:13)*

"My Son never once said, to my knowledge, while hanging on the cross, 'I thought they loved me... really loved me!' He said, 'Father, forgive them!' But instead of accepting his forgiveness, you stay focused on those voices, talking to you, and taunting you in your head, nagging you, and nagging you, as Delilah did my Samson."

"When satan taunts you with the images of war, counteract with images of my Son's love for you. He was crowned with thorns upon his head. This crown pierced his mind with the pain of the oppression of *my people*. He was pierced for the suicidal thoughts that enter *my people's* minds. He was pierced for the depressed minds of *my people* in order to set them free from all the oppression that enters the minds of *my people*."

"You haven't done that, have you? Yet you give in to the voices, and images, that Satan taunts you with, thus making you go in a direction you shouldn't go....away from me, the Lord your God! All of you at one time in your life, from all walks of life, have been taunted by satan and his arsenal against you, in his efforts to get you to abandon your faith in me, the Lord your God!"

"The minute you give in to the taunting of satan, the enemy of your soul, all hell will break loose on you, and in your life. Then you will be totally convinced that I, the Lord your God, have abandoned you, and forgotten you."

"Therefore I say to you,

"Be strong and courageous. Do not be afraid or terrified because of them, for the Lord your God goes with you; he will never leave you nor forsake you." *(Deuteronomy 31:6)*

CHAPTER FIVE

Samson's Fall

"There is not a single soul on the face of the earth that has not had a failure of any kind in their life, whether big or small."

"Then she (Delilah) *said to him; How can you say; I love you, when you won't confide in me? This is the third time you have made a fool of me and haven't told me the secret of your great strength." "With such nagging she prodded him day after day until he was sick to death of it. So he told her everything. No razor has ever been used in my head, he said, because I have been a Nazarite dedicated to God from my mother's womb. If my head were shaved my strength would leave me and I would become as weak as any other man. When Delilah saw that he had told her everything, she sent word to the rulers of the Philistines. "Come back once more, he has told me everything. So the rulers of the Philistines returned with the silver in their hands. After putting him to sleep on her lap, she called for someone to shave off the seven braids of his hair, and so begin to subdue him. And his strength left him! Then she called, "Samson", the Philistines are upon you. He awoke from his sleep and thought, I'll go out as before and shake myself free. But he didn't know the Lord had left him."* (Judges 16:15-20)

"As an individual, one can only take so much pressure on the level of their resistance. Some people have more patience than others. Some can go further than others while going the extra mile. But sooner, or later, the resistance of temptation and endurance snaps. As one, you try to do what is right, while totally being surrounded by evil and wrong doing."

"I do not understand what I do. For what I want to do, I do not do, but what I hate I do." *(Romans 7:15)*

"It's not always being tempted with evil behavior that is to be considered as sin. Another form of temptation is considered peer pressure. That is when you are challenged to do something that isn't even in your nature, or in your personality, to do. You are not even close to being a drunk, nor has it ever crossed your mind. You are just a casual drinker, one who drinks on special occasions, or in times of celebration. But then you find yourself in the midst of a people who love to get drunk every chance they get. So they challenge you!"

"You give in, just to fit in. You get high and wasted on drugs just to fit in. Another is just simple behavior tactics people do to one another. They try to out-do each other, out-dress each other, and live a life they really can't afford; but, they are only doing it to make it seem like they can. There is even peer pressure in trying to do the right things the Lord would have you do unto other people, while noticing you are not even appreciated."

"What the hell?"

"My command is this: Love *each other as I have* loved *you."* *(John 15:12)*

"The simple answer is: Love conquers all! It's hard to believe that love is the answer to my freedom from this world's heartaches, sorrows and hopelessness! It's as though you can barely find love for yourself from all the others around you in this life you live."

"I have a lot of people tell me they love me -- family, friends, and even acquaintances. But I guess my soul searching goes deeper than just being told by those who do really care for me, Lord. What's wrong with me?

Am I just selfish? Nothing seems to soothe my soul to the point of obtaining peace and rest within my being."

"You do remember the restaurant buffet I mentioned earlier to you, don't you? You choose what you want and eat it, and then pay for it. Well, sometimes the love you are looking for requires for you to give it to others. These might be people you wouldn't even imagine giving it to."

"And who might that be? Love doesn't always require you to **not hate** people in your life. Sometimes, love requires you to forgive those who hurt you, or those who ruined your life. But I want you to understand - just because you forgive someone who hurt you does not mean you have to accept that person back into your life, as they are. Some people will never change their character and being, even if their life depended on it, even if you forgive them! They just will not change! They will go to their graves being who they are."

"So why forgive them?"

"Because, by doing so, you can set yourself free from the grip of these spirits of hell that have ruined your life, that's why! You're not doing **them** a favor. You're doing **yourself** a HUGE favor!"

"Once you can conquer that mountain in your life you don't seem to want to climb, your next obstacle is to be able to forgive yourself for something you did. Forgive yourself for something you allowed, that you never really intended to do to someone, or yourself, in the first place."

"People who are affected by the forgiveness realm of God are not always people who don't care to do anything right in their lives - those unwilling to change their ways. However, in general, a sinner is one who does everything they are not supposed to do, according to the word of God. That includes every human being on the face of the earth."

"So we are not looking for perfection, as I told you earlier, in order for me, the Lord your God, to help you. I AM talking to righteous people, those who long to do the right things according to my word, although everything in their personal lives has seemed to have gone wrong."

"These people are nowhere near perfect, only forgiven of me," says the Lord, "with the intention of not losing their faith in me, as they hold onto my promise of eternal life in my kingdom of heaven."

"You can be one of those, too, if you would just allow me to do in your life what needs to be done. I promise you, you will see my Son's love for you when we finish this conversation."

"Righteous people are those who try and live a happy and righteous life, to the best of their God given ability, and faith through his word."

"Clearly no one who relies on the law is justified before God, because, '...the righteous will live by faith.'" *(Galatians 3:11)*

"But my righteous one will live by faith. And I take no pleasure in the one who shrinks back." *(Hebrews 10:38)*

"Did you notice I said, 'I take no pleasure in the one who shrinks back'? It means I AM ready to help you, *my child*! I AM ready to help you, America! I AM here this very day, in your presence, to forever change your life, and your country," says the Lord!

"Why?"

"Because you have become the victims of satan's spiritual attacks on you, and your nation," says the Lord. "You have become the victims of crime, and murders, racism, hate, prejudice, and injustices. You have been sexually assaulted and violated. You have been physically and mentally abused by the wickedness of satan's kingdom of darkness."

"You are the casualties of divorce and separation of families. You are now in the midst of a no-morality society, one where everything evil seems good, while everything righteous seems evil. I AM speaking to the youth and young adults of this depraved, ripped-off society," says the

Lord. "You and your children hold the future in your hands, a future that can forever be changed, if you will allow me to heal your broken hearts, and shattered lives," says the Lord.

"I AM speaking of the children and the young adults of this generation, those who are looking for a leader to follow. They have this drive in them that says, "Regardless of everything going on around me that seems hopeless, I know there's got to be more to life than what I AM seeing!"

"I AM he that you are searching for, *my child*," says the Lord. "Just don't tell me with a lying heart, 'I will follow you wherever you go, Lord! Because, then, I will tell you what I told another person who told me that same statement when I walked the face of the earth:

"Then a teacher of the law came to him and said, "Teacher, I will follow you any place you go." Jesus said to him, "Foxes have holes to live in. The birds have nests. But the Son of Man has no place to rest."
(Matthew 8:19-20 ERV)

"In others words, you cannot sleep while following me."

"What?"

"I AM not speaking of natural sleep. I AM simply saying you must be alert, and stay alert, always in your life in me. This must be, in order for me to operate in you, and through you, to help you overcome all the adversity that comes against you in your life."

"Didn't I just mention forgiveness to you a while ago, forgive those who hurt you? What did you do when you read that? Your mind went numb, instinctively, and rejected my advice. Yet you said, 'I'll do that later, after I finish reading this message God has for me…if it's what I want.'"

"That is why you were told at the very beginning of this message, 'Keep your mind on Christ Jesus, my Son.' This is about his love for you, his desire to help you in healing your broken heart and shattered life. This is about his love for you, America, your broken hearts, and shattered

American lives."

"But, I know I have '*my Samsons*', who, against all odds, keep pushing forward in this life, though they are deeply wounded within. Mention forgiveness to them, and you may need to step back. They are the ones that the voices of the Delilah spirits taunt day and night, night and day, every day and every hour of their lives. The satanic voices traumatize them by saying, 'Do what everybody else does! That's how everybody deals with their personal issues in life. Don't worry about what anyone thinks! You know you carry so much anger, and unforgiveness in you, that God's words will come back to haunt you.'"

"Karma? Is that what it's called? Satan will use my very word to throw confusion into the minds of *my people*," says the Lord. He will speak of the words Jesus Christ spoke to the people:

"But I say, if you are even angry with someone, you are subject to judgement! If you call someone an idiot, you are in danger of being brought before the court. And if you curse someone, you are in danger of the fires of hell."   (Matthew 5:22 NLT)

"The voice of the enemy of your souls, satan, says,

'It seems as though your God in heaven, the one you love and worship so much, cares more about those who hurt you than you, the one who is wounded and hurt. For God says you can't be angry because he will judge you! You can't be name calling, because he will judge you in his court. And if you curse someone, you will go to hell to be with me, the prince of darkness!

'So, if you ask me, it's a lost cause for you in your efforts of finding your healing, your forgiveness, and your hope you have in God your creator, who made you in his image. Something very drastic will have to take place in order for restoration to even begin.

'Those that hurt you did what they wanted to do to you, and got away with it. And now all God asks, is for you to forgive them? Really! Is that the loving God you serve, and believe in?

'Is that why you stay with a man who physically beats you, and verbally abuses you mentally with insults, and persecutions? You walk around like you are made of glass that any wrong move you make will shatter your being into a million little pieces, knowing you will be beat by your lover.

'Your boss; the pimp! Your drug lord! Your homies! Your clique! Or your woman, who loves you just for your paychecks. You say, 'So long as I see her smile, and it makes her happy, it makes me happy.' Yet, you're miserable as hell within your own spirit and being. Has God's love blinded you so much, that you can't see it's your hard-earned money that makes her happy, that has nothing to do with you as a person?

'Or your boyfriend, who uses you for room and board while having a place to eat, and just someone to have sex with. That makes you happy, while helping you deal with your insecurity, and fear of being lonely. You're lonely as hell already, even with that pervert in your life.

'Is that why you cry at night over your children? You do everything in love as a father, or a mother, or even a relative should do, including giving forgiveness? Yet they go about their own self-centered lives, in their own selfishness, with no regard or care about your life.

'And you fathers and mothers who prayed for your sick child that the Lord didn't heal! How can you say you love the God of heaven? You are living your life in anger and resentment. You hate everything, and everyone, around you. You even hate your own life!

'That's why everybody else around you does what they do! They're in the same boat as you, dealing with the same, rough waters of the seas that God created for all of you to be in... except you keep trying to hold onto God as the captain of your ship.

'Not them! They control their own ships! That's my job as the prince of this world, and the prince of the underworld! To get you to see that your

God doesn't really care about you! He allowed all this to happen to you. Just tell me the secret of your strength, amidst all this adversity in your life, and I will leave you alone.'"

"Satan's mission… He wants to know the secret of your strength," says God.

Satan continues, 'Look at you! You're wasted, and hooked on drugs and alcohol. You're depressed, with a mind consumed with oppression. You're convinced you'd rather be dead than to have to deal with all this misery, heartache, and sorrow this life is full of. You're actually dead already to the world around you, though you are alive and walking around them, yet totally unnoticed!

'And what's your heart's desire? To be like Jesus Christ, more than a conqueror over death and the darkness of this world. That way, you can be an instrument of God to help save and reach a dying and hurting world. Not to mention the healing of diseases, and sicknesses amidst all of you, healings that you have never experienced. You need to help yourself before worrying about anybody else in and around your life.'"

"How can you be a child of the Most High God, in this mindset? It is obvious satan has taken *my people* to the point of revealing their secret, just as he did Samson through Delilah. You have literally forgotten that amidst everything that your life has turned out to be, I still have the very number of hairs on your head all numbered," says the Lord. "I still have my mighty hand upon you, America!"

"So I see you have given in to the voices of Delilah. Now you have fallen asleep in Delilah's lap, relieved of the peer pressure tormenting your hearts, souls and minds. So now you find this law at work in your very own lives. This law is at work in the very core of your nation," says the Lord.

"Although I want to do good, evil is right there with me. For in my inner being I delight in God's law, but I see another law at work in me, waging war against the law of my mind making me a prisoner of the law of sin at

work within me. What a wretched man I AM! Who will rescue me from this body that is subject to death?"   *(Romans 7:21-24)*

(Meditation prayer)

I couldn't go anymore, Lord! I AM so sorry! It has been so hard on me, O Lord, and I just couldn't find someone to lean on and talk to. I know you love me, and you have the very number of hairs in my head all numbered. But I can't seem to feel you, O Lord, much less see you to hold you, and cry with you in your loving arms, O Lord.

It's hard to forgive others for what they've done to me, O Lord. I have a hard time forgiving myself for what I have done. I'm scared, God! I feel so alone in this great, big world I AM living in, that consists of billions of people, yet I feel so alone. The mindset, and mental anguish my mind, body and soul go through is almost unbearable. It affects every area of my life, even when I try to be positive and optimistic. I even look at people who are far worse off than me, and that makes me be very thankful to you for all my blessings, that I try not to take for granted. Even then, satan won't let up about how I gave in to my weaknesses, and let go of my faith in you, O Lord.

I miss my loved ones so much who have been gone, when I should be thanking you for putting them into my life in the first place. God, help me, O Lord! Have mercy on me, and my soul! Don't abandon me in my failures like everyone else has. Lord, remember me when your kingdom comes. And let your will be done in my life, as it is in heaven. Let your will be done in our great nation of America, as it is in heaven. Amen!

"I have told you these things, so that in me you may have peace. In this world you will have trouble. But take heart! I have overcome the world."
                                                                       (John 16:33)

"After Jesus said this, he looked toward heaven and prayed: Father, the hour has come. Glorify your Son, that your Son may glorify you. For you

granted him authority over all people that he might give eternal life to all those you have given him. Now this is eternal life: that they know you, the <u>ONLY</u> true God, and Jesus Christ, whom you have sent. I have brought you glory on earth by finishing the work you gave me to do. And now, Father, glorify me in your presence with the glory I had with you before the world began."   *(John 17:1-5)*

CHAPTER SIX

Samson's Defeat

If I could find a living soul who has never hit rock bottom over a failure, or a let-down in his own personal life, I would love to meet him, and allow him to counsel me in my life's heartaches, sorrows, and defeats.

"Then the Philistines seized him, gouged out his eyes and took him with bronze shackles, they set him to grinding grain in the prison."
(Judges 16:21)

"Samson endured total physical and mental torture for giving away the secret of his supernatural strength. Imagine the pain, and the anguish, of being attacked, beaten, and overpowered, while having your eyes gouged out of their sockets; then left for dead. In all honesty, just about every one of you in the midst of humanity can relate to that pain, from an emotional and spiritual level. You are wearing emotional and spiritual inner scars, that if you could trade them for physical scars, you would!"

"Physical pain involving abuse go away eventually, but not the inner pain, and memories of the abuse itself. No physician in this world can heal the pain that brings more tears out of one's soul, more tears than any physical pain can."

"It is so obvious! Right before your very eyes in sporting competitions, you will see an athlete get hurt and fall to the ground in terrible pain, and physical anguish; yet, very few cry tears during that physical pain. However, let a loved one of that athlete pass away, and even though it doesn't affect the physical body, it will bring tears of pain from within."

"Either way, whether it goes away or not, the inner pain of the soul and the spirit hurts more, since they are lodged into the heart, soul, and the mind of mankind. Sexual assault of rape, indecent acts committed against you, physical and emotional abuse and total rejection in your lives have all allowed satan to gouge your eyes out of their sockets. This is because you have given in to his taunting, and have assumed the guilt and responsibility for what has happened to you and your life."

"Regardless, even though Samson's eyes were gouged out, he was still alive. If I was the hateful God I AM made out to be, I should have just let them take Samson out, and go ahead and kill him, once and for all."

"That goes for you, too! You may say, 'He might as well have been dead, with his eyes gouged out!'"

"Really! You are still very much alive, and living, except with no vision of a future for yourself. You are in total darkness in your life, having your eyes gouged out by satan, since you revealed your secret to the Delilah spirit."

"Samson was totally annihilated and defeated, yet still alive. He was in total despair, hopeless, and suffering greatly within his being… **Just as you are at this very moment in your life**! Just as you are as a nation!"

"Now, the emptiness and darkness, the loneliness and confusion, mixed with fear, rule your life as they did my Samson. On top of all of this is the weight of guilt, burdening you with an invisible weight on your soul and spirit that no eye can see. Even your physical body can feel the weight, and the burden, of the tormenting guilt and regret within your soul, and being."

"That's why I told *my people*,

"Come to me, all you who are weary and burdened, and I will give you rest." (Matthew 11:28)

"Yet, they refuse to believe I can help!"

"A cheerful heart is good medicine, but a crushed spirit dries up the bones." (Proverbs 17:22)

"There isn't really much you have to be thankful about after what has happened in your life, is there? The loss of a loved one, especially at such a young age! The loss of a marriage to unfaithfulness, after giving up everything, and everyone, for that marriage. Your children have gone their own way, while the whole time, you thought they would drop in pretty regularly to visit you. They chose a road, or a lifestyle, you would never have ever imagined them doing, one that you would rather have not seen, or had to deal with."

"Now, you have given up on yourself, and given up on your faith in me, the Lord your God, because of the total blindness that has consumed you. You have had your eyes gouged out of their sockets. That's why a lot of you have become addicts to your addictions, your drugs and your alcohol!"

"You are now imprisoned by medications to deal with your anxiety attacks on your nerves. You've become a prisoner to depression, oppression, and loneliness, topped off with fear and insecurity. You've become a prisoner, just as Samson became a prisoner, one who could not physically see anymore, no matter where he was taken, or where he was led. He just went wherever he was taken, by those who had control of him, and his life. Even if he spoke out to say he didn't want to go there anymore, he was totally powerless to control where he was taken."

"This is exactly like you! You are talking to your drugs and alcohol, while crying in tears, saying to your addictions, 'I'm so tired of this! I don't want you anymore!' Yet you are overpowered by the power of the spirit of your addictions."

"You cry to your children, saying, 'I can't help you anymore! Help yourself!' Yet you are overpowered by the tears that well up in their eyes, tears that soften your heart to give in to their demands. If not, fear overpowers you in thinking they won't come to see you anymore if they don't get what they want. Yet in reality, that is the only time they do come see you, if they're in need!"

"Total blindness on your part, by having your eyes gouged out. This is satan's mastermind tactics against your faith in me, the Lord your God, who has all the very hairs of your head all numbered."

"You cry to your abusive partner, or spouse, 'Stop this torture! Please!' But the fear of them overpowers you and your will to live. Total pitch darkness, and hopelessness."

"Your fears and insecurities even lead to a table, or a couch, in the wee hours of the night, where you sit and cry your eyes out, while holding your head between your hands, as though your head is about to explode. You even cry from within your desperate soul, 'GOD! Where are you?'"

"The spirits even take you to bed, as you cry yourself to sleep over all the defeats and let-downs this life has given you, wishing you didn't have to wake up the next day. What else can a person do who has had their eyes gouged out, leaving them totally blind?"

"The Spirit gives life, the flesh counts for nothing. The words I have spoken to you – they are full of Spirit and life." (John 6:63)

"Though I AM talking about literal eyes being gouged out of their sockets, I AM speaking of the vision you have of your life that is unseen; though you have eyes to see with, yet you don't see," says the Lord! "All you can see is total darkness and hopelessness, America!"

"If a nation is not guided by God, the people will lose self-control, but the nation that obeys God's law will be happy." (Proverbs 29:18 ERV)

"My son! My daughter!"

Where there is no vision, (no revelation of God and his word) the people are unrestrained: but happy is he who keeps the law (of God)."
(Proverbs 29:18 AMP)

"He told them, the secret of the kingdom of God has been given to you. But to those on the outside everything is said in parables, so that, "they may be ever seeing, but never perceiving, and ever hearing, but never understanding, otherwise they might turn and be forgiven."
(Mark 4:11-12)

"So, as the Philistines took Samson, bound up in shackles of bronze, they set him up to grind grain in prison. Can you imagine going from being the strongest human on the face of the earth, to one who was over powered and taken to prison, to grind grain with all the other slaves in prison?"

"At one time you looked down on people who were imprisoned to fears, hopelessness, addictions, and everything else you said with your breath that you would never do. Now, you're a prisoner just like them. Just think of what they were doing in prison. They were grinding up grain into flour, for it to be prepared for the elite of the kingdom of the Philistines."

"Is that what you are doing in your life, now that you have totally lost your vision in your own life's future? Grinding your will, just to survive this life you are living? Grinding your finances just to get your next meal, or rent where you won't end up in a homeless shelter, or with family, since your drinking and drugs have you imprisoned? Grinding your thoughts on how you can get your next high, or drunk?"

"Even if it's stealing from your loved ones, just to support your addictions, thus feeding your suppliers of booze and drugs, while you starve yourself, and your family. Keeping the drug lords and dealers happy, the kings of the Philistine kingdom, that have you as a slave-driven prisoner."

"How about your ex-husband, or your ex-wife? Are you grinding them to powder, using your children as weapons of retaliation, just because things didn't work out between the two of you? Do you grind your husband or your wife to death over the broken heartedness, and disappointment your own children have brought you? You even had your son, or your daughter serve your country, and that doesn't mean a thing to anyone you."

"What about you followers of mine, who say you love me, yet you grind everybody else around you with condemnation because of how they live? For I know you are in prison because of your weaknesses and defeats in your life. Does that give you the right to grind everything, and everyone, around you and your life, into powder that can be blown away with a light breeze?"

"Then, you wonder why your churches are empty! You wonder why America is in a spiraling downfall in its morality, or even in its caring level. I totally blame you, the churches, for the falling away of *my people*," says the Lord!

"You even wonder why you have very few people in and around your personal life. It's because of the choices you have made in dealing with your own failures. You have been taken prisoner, and now you have become a slave to the Philistine's (satan's) kingdom, only to do as you're told by the voices of darkness."

"Now the rulers of the Philistines assembled to offer a great sacrifice to Dagon their God and to celebrate, saying, 'Our God has delivered Samson, our enemy, into our hands.'"

"When the people saw him, they praised their God, saying, our God has delivered our enemy into our hands, the one who laid waste our land and multiplied our slain."

"While they were in high spirits, they shouted, "Bring out Samson to entertain us. So they called Samson out of the prison and he performed for them. When they stood him among the pillars." *(Judges 16:23-25)*

"Now, everybody who wanted to see you fall and fail has gotten their wish. They celebrate their victory over your life, paying homage to their 'god' saying, 'Our god of envy, jealousy, anger, and unforgiveness is against this child of God in heaven, who has been delivered into our hands. This nation of God's (America) has been given over to us through their fear of terrorism and an immoral society! Let's celebrate!'"

"While they are in high spirits, they shout out, "Bring us this Samson (child of God) out to entertain us. Bring out this nation of God's (America) out to entertain us!'"

"So they called Samson (*my people*) out of prison, and he performed for them: public intoxications; armed robberies and violent assaults while they are high on drugs; sexually perverted acts, and performances non-stop; and bullying, leading to many young lives committing suicide."

"They called out, 'Bring out Samson (America) out of prison to perform for us!' So, America performed for the world to see: passing same sex marriage laws; kicking God out of schools and classrooms; removing Ten Commandment monuments all over their nation; wars of hate, and prejudice, wars of racism, and injustices against innocent people; the gunning down of innocent lives, and police officers; violent street demonstrations of all types in the areas of politics and law."

"The spirit of Samson was over powered by the spirit of the nagging and deceptive Delilah that caused the downfall of *my chosen one*. He fell in love with a lying, deceitful woman, one he trusted, just as many have fallen in love with a deceitful woman I call, **the church of religion and denominations.**"

"The body of Christ? That's what you call yourselves? You do to *my people* as Delilah did to Samson, except you go opposite of what Delilah did. Delilah wanted to know what the secret was to Samson's strength. You, on the other hand, want to know what my hurting people's weakness is, before you even think of helping them. You already know the secret of their weakness, but you insist on knowing the source of their weakness, to humiliate them, in an effort to make them feel guilty. This is so they can bow before you at your altar of the church, and the altar of your religion."

"Are your altars better than my Son's sacrificial altar he took upon himself on the cross? You're asking them to give you a performance of repentance, and sorrow, before you even have mercy on their darkened, defeated souls."

"I say to you, 'Repent of your wickedness, before you are called out of me, the Lord your God, after your eyes get gouged out through your own ignorance, leading you to perform your disgrace before those you won't have mercy on."

"Jesus said: For judgement I have come into the world, so that the blind would see and those who see would become blind. Some of the Pharisees who were with him heard him say this and asked: What? Are we blind too? Jesus said: If you were blind, you would not be guilty of sin, but now that you claim you can see, your guilt remains."   *(John 9:39-41)*

"You people, my church, haven't the slightest idea of how you have turned *my people* against me, with your laws of religion and Christianity, not to mention the names of religions, faiths, and denominations. I would say *my hurting people* are better off sitting in a graveyard meditating with me, than they would be in a hypocritical environment full of condemnation, instead of love and forgiveness."

"You do to my dying world like the self-centered Philistines did to my Samson. They celebrated his fall and his defeat. You do that by looking down on my hurting, lost world by wanting judgments of destruction on people who are not perfect like you."

"They're all going to hell anyway!"

"How would you know? I don't think you are too sure about your own salvation, at times, in your own personal life. There's only one way to be sure! You will see how at the end of my message to you," says the Lord.

"So they brought Samson out of prison and he performed for them, when they stood him *"among the pillars"*. Now you're the life of the party. You're now the source in people's lives of drugs, alcohol, sex, and perversion. Free lifestyle living, and having fun the whole time you are imprisoned to yourself. Babysitting your children's children, unpaid for your services, while paying all their debts off for them, since you didn't want to see them struggle the same way you did to earn your keep."

"The whole time you are performing in front of them. You think they are enjoying you amidst the laughter and celebration of what life is all about. Yet in reality, it's the spirits of hell who are laughing at you, and enjoying your performance at their command. They're laughing at your defeated spirit that is the cause of you really having no life left in you. You're doing all this amidst the pillars they stood you among, just as they did my Samson."

"REMEMBER the pillars! Why do I say that?"

"Regardless, you have had your eyes gouged out, and you are in total darkness. Yet, I assure you,

"No weapon that has been made to be used against you will succeed. You will have an answer for anyone who accuses you. This is the inheritance of the Lord's servants. Their victory comes from me, declares the Lord." (Isaiah 54:17 GWT)

"Lord! How can you say in your own word, 'No weapon that has been made to be used against me will succeed'? My eyes have just been gouged out, and I AM in total darkness over all the choices I've made in my life. Our eyes have been gouged out over all the terrorist attacks we have been plagued with, God. Even the injustice in our nation, Lord, has literally ruined millions of lives. We are totally defeated as 'the America' we once were. I AM totally defeated with no vision of hope in sight. Total darkness! Help us, O Lord!"

"I told you in the beginning of this message," says the Lord, "to keep your mind on my Christ! Even if you have to refocus your mind, even now, after all you have read. The only reason you have come this far is *my word* is alive in you! Even though you are where you are in your life story this very moment, my word is alive in you."

"As *my child*, <u>NEVER</u> forget! As *my chosen nation*, America! <u>NEVER</u> forget! As *my church*, <u>NEVER</u> forget!"

"I can do all things through Christ who strengthens me."
(Philippians 4:13 NKJV)

"Even in the midst of total darkness, blindness, and defeat!"

CHAPTER SEVEN

Samson's Death

"Darkness plagues the lives of *my people* in this United States of America," says the Lord. "As dark as it has gotten over the years, and as blind as America has become by those who gouged her eyes out, the light still shines in the darkness of this nation," says the Lord. "As dark as it has gotten in your life, and as blind as you have been left by those who gouged your eyes out, leaving you in total darkness *my child*,

"In him was life, and that life was the light of all mankind." *(John 1:4)*

"I AM speaking of my Son, Jesus Christ, the one you were told to stay focused on when you first began to read my message to you. Regardless of what happened to Samson in his life, I never allowed the enemy to take him out, literally. He was still alive! Just as you are, even though it has crossed your mind to take yourself out quite a few times already, as others have. But I, the Lord your God, haven't allowed the enemy, satan, to be successful in that area of your life. In fact, I have never allowed the enemy to succeed in anyone's life in that area. You through your own reasoning ultimately have the last say so in making your own choices in this life you live."

"Samson still had a spirit of life within him that I, the Lord his God, had given him – the same spirit I have given you, *my child*, and the same spirit I have given you, America! I told you, I have heard the cries of your miseries," says the Lord! "For even amidst such despair, hopelessness, and humiliation, I can hear the sincerity of *my people* in this chosen nation of mine."

"Therefore, say to the Israelites (America, *my people*): I AM *the Lord, and I will bring you out from under the yoke of the Egyptians* (Philistines, your enemies). *I will free you from being slaves to them, and I will redeem you with an outstretched arm and with mighty acts of judgment."* *(Exodus 6:6)*

"Will you, O Lord?"

"Yes, I will, *my child*! Yes, I will, America! Though the promise just given pertained to my servant Moses at that time, it was for my servant Samson who faced the Philistines in his day, just as you face the devil in this day and age."

"I AM, the God of Moses! I AM, the God of Samson! I AM your God, *my child*, just as I AM the God of your nation, America! There isn't a place on this earth, or even in the deepest part of hell, I cannot deliver *my people* from," says the Lord!"

"Even though everyone has given up on you, America, I will never give up on you," says the Lord. "You've been criticized and ridiculed. You've even been condemned to hell! I have heard the very words that have been spoken against you as a nation, satan's declaration to your nation: 'Death to America!' The same applies for the people of this great nation. I have never condemned you America, because I love you," says the Lord.

"For God did not send his Son into the world to condemn the world, but to save the world through him." *(John 3:17)*

"My Son is about to fulfill those words right before your very eyes, since you have lost your vision. I AM about to bring light back into your darkened lives, America! I AM about to bring healing to your wounded and broken hearts, deliver you from your imprisonments of oppression and depression that are embedded in the very depths of your hearts, souls and minds," says the Lord.

"Although Samson fell victim to deception and betrayal, after giving in to the pressure of a taunting voice that led him into slavery, humiliation, and total defeat, satan overlooked the one very important aspect of Samson's life that was right before his eyes. It is an aspect in your own life that you yourself have totally overlooked, though it was right before your very own eyes. It's an aspect that you as a nation have literally overlooked in your time of deception, betrayal and defeat, by allowing immoral laws to be passed, while celebrating them with great pleasure… SAMSON'S HAIR GREW BACK!"

"But his hair started to grow back as soon as it was shaved off."
(Judges 16:22 GWT)

"You realize when his hair grew back? As soon as it was shaved off! The minute you gave your secret away, your hair started growing back. The minute you were overpowered by peer pressure, your hair was growing back. The minute you felt defeated by betrayal, and deception, your hair was growing back. Your hair was already growing back when you had your eyes gouged out, and your vision was taken from you."

"I still could have told you the number of hairs on your head, just by the simple roots left on you, after the hair of your head was shaved. Even now, in the pit of hell you think you're in, I can tell you the number of hairs on your head. I have never forsaken you," says the Lord!

"There's a huge difference between leaving you, and forsaking you. Leaving you was my way of stepping out of the way, to allow the free will I gave you, when I created you, to work its way through your life, America. Even though you have revealed the secret of your strength, in more ways than one to the world, through the Delilah spirits you have within your own government, of greed, corruption, and betrayal, I AM still God over the United States of America!"

"I AM the God of your life, *my child*! Even in the midst of the pressure of people's rights being violated, through the passing of immoral laws to please the people of the land, instead of pleasing me, the Lord your God in heaven, America's hair has grown back!"

"And you, body of Christ! You have given your secret away, by compromising the gospel of my Son, Jesus Christ, with religion, faiths and denominations. That's why you get all caught up in all the worldly affairs going on around you. You become over powered by fear and insecurity issues, when all you were asked to do was PRAY! But, instead, you have taken your eyes off of me," says the Lord, "as terrorist acts occur right before your very eyes."

"Immoral laws are passed and approved right underneath your noses. Then you get consumed with judgmental spirits, condemning everyone and everything around you, thus totally forgetting, I still have the very hairs on your head all numbered."

"Therefore, you yourselves, as my body of believers, have lost your supernatural strength in overcoming all your fears and doubts, for the simple reason of being weak in the midst of evil."

"You say: *'And lead us not into temptation, but deliver us from the evil one.'"* *(Matthew 6:13)*

"What are you saying to me? Do you want me to keep you from the temptation of doing evil? That's what most of you desire, and that's great!"

"However, evil covers more than just literal things that would tempt you. Evil also includes activities going on all around you that you get all caught up in: racial issues and the passing of immoral laws. This does nothing more than rouse you up in your hearts, getting you filled with anger, hate, prejudice, and condemnation, while literally taking your eyes off of me, the Lord your God!"

"It comes from within the body of believers, like a cancer on a physical body that looks good on the outside, while it is being eaten away on the inside. What does one do when a physical body gets sick enough where it needs medical attention? He goes to a doctor, or a physician! You have heard the saying, 'Physician, heal yourself (Luke 4:23).' Right?"

"You, therefore, have no excuse, you who pass judgement on someone else, for at whatever point you judge another, you are condemning yourself, because you who pass judgement do the same things."
(Romans 2:1)

"So, the healing to this sickness in the body of Christ lies within your own reach. It's right in front of you! It's been there the whole time."

"When Samson got one last breath of hope, after realizing his hair had grown back, he did one more act of faith in his life. This is all you need to do as *my child*, my nation, and my body of believers, the church! He called on his servant <u>WHO HELD HIS HAND</u>!"

"Samson said to the servant who held his hand; Put me where I can feel the pillars that support the temple, that I may lean against them."
(Judges 16:26)

"You can only imagine the sorrow and the unrest Samson was burdened with in his soul. Giving his God-given secret away to his enemies; being overpowered by the enemies that he once ruled over; total defeat!"

"The unrest we are talking about is not only a physical tiredness, but an emotional restlessness, that of no peace whatsoever within his soul, just as most of you are now, as I speak," says the Lord. A physical tiredness of the body can be cured, as the body gets its rest through sleep."

"This is similar to what you do in your churches, which is why my Holy Spirit isn't allowed to do his work within his own body! This is what the body of believers has been doing over the years, sleeping and resting! Totally convinced I will punish the nations for evil and sin, through judgments I will send upon the face of the earth because of them."

"If I do, do you not think it would affect you? Oh! Yes, that's right, you are protected by the blood of Jesus! If you were, my Son's blood would cleanse you of your evil-hearted attitudes towards a dying, and hurting world."

"I specifically told you in **my word**:

"...and I AM very angry with the nations that feel secure. I was only a little angry, but they went too far with the punishment. Therefore this is what the Lord says: 'I will return to Jerusalem with mercy, and there 'my house' will be rebuilt. And the measuring line will be stretched out over Jerusalem,' declares the Lord Almighty." (Zechariah 1:15-16)

"I will have mercy on anyone who will come to me, as I just promised! But a measuring line has been drawn, just as it was at the beginning of time, a line that says: I AM God! You are not!"
"I the Lord do not change. So you, the descendants of Jacob, are not destroyed." (Malachi 3:6)

"I even came to earth to show you, *my people*, my love for you."

"Jesus Christ is the same yesterday and today and forever.
(Hebrews 13:8)

"I told you 'Keep your mind on Christ Jesus, my Son!' You are about to see his love in your life, as I have been saying that you would, through this entire message."

"That is why I want you to get up, stop sleeping and resting through your physical bodies as followers of mine. When one sleeps from tiredness in the physical body, he will awaken physically rested; but, the inward and unsettled restlessness still dominates your soul and being."

"The righteous people of God are tired of crying over unborn babies being taken out, before they even see the light of day in this world. They are crying over the bloodshed through acts of violence in the streets, public schools and neighborhoods. They are crying because innocent people and children are being gunned down over acts of hatred and prejudice. They are tired of racism and hateful attitudes about human life itself in this great nation, the United States of America!"

"That is why it is written for you followers of mine,

"That is why it is said: WAKE UP, O SLEEPER, rise from the dead, and Christ will shine on you."   *(Ephesians 5:14)*

"In the darkest hours of his life, Samson, through an act of faith, called on his servant for help. Who this servant was, or who it is, is not important to me," says the Lord. "Jesus Christ, my Son, is your servant, *my child*! Jesus Christ, my Son, is your servant, America! Jesus said to all of you:

"For who is greater, the one who is at the table or the one who serves? Is it not the one at the table? But I AM *among you as one who serves."*
          (Luke 22:27)

"As his creator, the Lord God of heaven and earth, I never took Samson's gift of strength from him, my chosen servant. Likewise, as God your creator, I would never take your gift from you, **Eternal Life**! That is the source of your strength, that gives you hope, and peace, in this dying, and decaying world you are living in."

"For the wages of sin is death, but <u>the gift of God</u> is eternal life in Christ Jesus, our Lord."   *(Romans 6:23)*

"For you, my body of Christ, know very well the wages of sin are death. So why do you take it upon yourselves to sentence *my people* to death over the sin in their lives? You very well know that it is written, if you condemn, you too will be condemned."

"Do not judge, and you will not be judged. Do not condemn, and you will not be condemned. Forgive and you will be forgiven."   *(Luke 6:37)*

"I would advise all of you to,
"Take delight in the Lord, and he will give you your heart's desire.

Commit everything you do to the Lord. Trust him, and he will help you."
(Psalm 37:4-5)

"As my body of believers, I know that you desire that everyone come into the knowledge, and unto the salvation, of the Lord Jesus Christ! It's my desire, too," says the Lord!

"The Lord is not slow in keeping his promise, as some understand slowness. Instead he is patient with you, not wanting anyone to perish, but everyone to come to repentance." *(2 Peter 3:9)*

"So delight yourself in me, the Lord your God, by committing yourself and everything you do, unto me," says the Lord. "Then <u>I WILL</u> help you! The same applies to you as a nation! The same applies to you as *my child* seeking help, and deliverance in your time of need."

"The secret of your strength has been revealed! Yet, even with that being done by millions, if not billions, who live in this world, I still have the very number of your hairs all numbered. Do not limit me, the Lord your God, with your own reasoning and thinking, through your own carnal minds."

"How terrible it will be for people who try hard to hide their plans from the Lord. They do their work in darkness. They think, 'Who sees us? Who will know?' They turn everything upside down. How silly they are to think that the potters are like the clay they work with. Can what is made say to the one who made it, 'You didn't make me?' Can the pot say to the potter, 'You don't know anything?'" *(Isaiah 29:15-16 NIVR)*

"Revealing your secret of being unable to forgive others, or even unable to forgive yourself, is the reason you are in the state of mind you are in the first place. Not to mention your insecurities of wanting to belong to something, or someone, just to fit in, and not feel left out."

"Always wanting more than what you already had, and not being content with what you do have, is another reason you gave the secret of your strength away to get-rich-quick schemes that only ripped you off. That's the reason you lost connection with your spouse, or even your children. No matter what anybody did, you were never satisfied, or content."

"But even in the midst of all this despair, I still have the very hairs of your head all numbered. I cannot give you what your heart desires, when your heart is full of anger, resentment, unforgiveness, and hatred towards everything, and everyone in your life. That is what brings on the darkness into your mind instead of the light of hope, love, and peace."

"Jesus spoke to the people once more and said, "I AM the light of the world. Whoever follows me will never walk in darkness, but will have the light of life." (John 8:12)

"So, if nothing else in your life right now, delight yourself in me, the Lord your God! Even if you don't feel worthy of it, just the fact I allowed your hair to grow back, and not a strand has been lost that I have counted, ought to be good enough for you to convince you that I have never forsaken you," says the Lord.

"So, now, *my child*, by finding some faith, even if it's just a little bit of faith, to call on me, as Samson did his servant, <u>EVERYTHING</u> in your life is about to change. EVERYTHING in your nation will forever change! EVERYTHING in the body of Christ will forever change! You just need to commit unto me everything you do, and trust me with it," says the Lord!

"Then I will help you, O child of mine! O church of mine! I will help you, America, beloved nation of mine, land of the free and home of the brave!"

"At your request, and as your servant, I will take you by the hands as you have asked me to, as did my servant Samson, since you can't see any more to get around, or even get ahead. I will do that for you, *my child*! I will do that for you, my church! I will do that for you, America!"

"Samson said to the servant who held his hand, Put me where I can feel

the pillars that support the temple, so that I may lean against them."
(Judges 16:26)

"The pillars! Yes, the support columns to the temple that held up the structure he was in. He asked to feel the pillars so he could rest upon them. Do you realize your body is the temple of God? I speak of your being, *my child*! Not your life, not your churches, or even your nation of America! Those are only what you are part of! You are not just part of me; you belong to me," says the Lord.

"Don't you realize that your body is the temple of the Holy Spirit, who lives in you and was given to you by God? You do not belong to yourself." *(1 Corinthians 6:19 NLT)*

"I AM speaking to you on a personal level now, whether you live for me, or not," says the Lord. "Throughout this whole message I have spoken to you as '*my child*', 'my church', and as 'my chosen nation of America'! But I AM about to fulfill my promise of love to you, in the darkness you are in, right now. That is why it is personal from here on out."

"The <u>ONLY</u> reason your life has turned out the way it has, is because you relied on your own strength, of trusting everyone, and everything else in and around your life, except me," says the Spirit of the Lord.

"The pillars that are supporting your temple, your life you are in right now, are two pillars that you control. One pillar is called '**SELF**', and the other pillar is called, '**WILL**'."

"**SELF-WILL** has been the upholding pillars in your lives, *my people*! Self-will has been the upholding source in the body of Christ! Self-will has been the upholding source to the United States of America! Since self-will has been the dominant force in your personal lives, it has infiltrated into your churches, your towns, and even in your big cities. It needs to be dealt with."

"Your self-wills have robbed you of your strength in me," says the Lord. "That is why your lives are so full of emptiness, heartbreak, and sorrow.

That is why your churches are empty and powerless. That is why your nation is full of violence, anger, racism, and bloodshed in the streets. There's only <u>ONE</u> remedy to what has happened in and around your life. Do what my defeated Samson did, in the midst of his greatest darkness and time of hopelessness. Ask me for your servant, my Son, the Lord Jesus Christ, to take you by the hand, and stand you among the pillars of your life, 'self-will'!"

"You realize the temple you are in is crowded and full of people who are watching you perform, as Samson did, after he gave the secret away of his strength."

"Now the temple was crowded with men and women, all the rulers of the Philistines were there, and on the roof were about three thousand men and women who were watching Samson perform."   *(Judges 16:27)*

"You have elevated yourself in this life to a position that has people talking and gossiping about you. They are laughing at you and ridiculing you as an individual, as a church, and even as a nation."

"Then Samson prayed to the Lord, "Sovereign Lord", remember me, <u>PLEASE</u>, God, strengthen me just once more, and let me with one blow get revenge on the Philistines for my two eyes."   *(Judges 16:28)*

"Take notice of what Samson did! <u>HE PRAYED</u>! Amidst total darkness and hopelessness, he prayed! Amidst total blindness, he prayed! In the midst of <u>TOTAL DEFEAT</u>, he prayed! You ought to do that as *my child*! You ought to do that as my church! You need to that unto me, as a nation," says the Lord.

"And when you pray, pray the prayer Samson prayed. He wanted revenge for his two eyes. He lost his sight in falling to his temptation, not being able to resist the evil that came at him through the voice of Delilah, the one he loved and trusted! He didn't want revenge on those who gouged his eyes out, or those who overpowered him! He wanted justice against his enemies who took his vision of his future.

"Why?"

"Without prophetic vision people run wild, but blessed are those who follow God's teachings."   *(Proverbs 29:18 GWT)*

"Samson prayed for strength from his God! The strongest man in the universe had no strength whatsoever to fight the evil spirits of darkness that had over powered his will to live. He called on his creator, the Lord God of heaven and earth! Why?"

"He gives strength to the weary and increases the power of the weak."
(Isaiah 40:29)

"At his request, Samson's servant did just as Samson asked him to do."

"Then Samson reached toward the two central pillars on which the temple stood. Bracing himself against them, his right hand on the one, and his left hand on the other."   *(Judges 16:29)*

The central pillars of your life, your churches, and your nation are what they stand on. It is what has supported your everyday activities and decisions you have made in your lives, which have turned out to be disastrous, <u>SELF-WILL</u>!"

"So, now, bracing yourself against those pillars in your life, position yourself to put your left hand on the pillar called SELF, and your right hand on the pillar called WILL!"

"The only difference in Samson's servant, in comparison to your servant, is his involvement in your request. Samson's servant placed Samson hands where he could feel the pillars."

"Your servant, my Son Jesus Christ, stands behind you as he places your left hand on the pillar called **SELF**, and your right hand on the pillar called **WILL**. Then, my Son, Jesus Christ places his left hand over your left hand braced against the pillar, thus turning the word, **SELF**, into <u>***HIS***</u>."

"My Son, Jesus Christ then places his right hand over your right hand over the word, **WILL**. Now, all I see from heaven," says the Lord, "are my Son's hands over yours, and it reads, *"Your kingdom come, your will be done, on earth as it is in heaven."* *(Matthew 6:10)*

"Your will be done in my life, Lord! In our churches, Lord! In our United States of America, Lord, as it is in heaven!"

CHAPTER EIGHT

A NEW BEGINNING

As the time drew near, I looked up into the heavens, and I felt my Savior Jesus Christ's hands over mine. I felt what seemed to be raindrops falling onto my forehead as I looked up. I envisioned God, my Father, crying tears of joy and happiness that I had whole-heartedly accepted my servant Jesus Christ's help in my life.

I spoke from within my soul to God, my Father, in heaven,

"I'm ready Lord! I am ready for change! I'm ready for restoration! I want a new beginning! I believe in you! Give me strength to push the self-will pillars out of my life, and into yours. I am totally ready for your Son, Jesus Christ, to help me overcome all my enemies, and change my life!"

"And a voice from heaven said, "This is my Son, whom I love, with him I AM well pleased." (Matthew 3:17)

"A voice came from the cloud, saying, "This is my Son, whom I have chosen, listen to him." (Luke 9:35)

"Jesus said, 'Father, forgive them, for they do not know what they are doing'. And they divided his clothes by casting lots." (Luke 23:34)

When heaven heard Jesus Christ's voice of forgiveness with his hands over mine, silence came over the entire kingdom of heaven. The silence poured itself out over the entire earth. Darkness came over the land.

"From noon until three in the afternoon darkness came over the land. About three in the afternoon Jesus cried out in a loud voice, "Eli, Eli, Lema sabachthani? (which means "My God, my God, why have you forsaken me?"). (Matthew27:45-46)

"My kingdom," says the Lord, "at that very instant, forsook my Son Jesus Christ, for what he took upon himself: *My people*'s rebellion against me, the Lord God of heaven and earth, who has the very number of your hairs all numbered."

"Samson saw only one way to justify his mistake of revealing his secret to the Delilah spirit, but it wasn't through vengeance against anyone, personally. It was more of a personal sacrifice of himself unto me, the Lord his God, for what he personally felt he did. He felt that he let me down under the pressure, from the non-stop, continuous nagging and begging from someone very close to him. So he gave himself to me as an act of faith, and said 'Let me die with the Philistines!'"

"Now, you do as Samson did, and say what Samson said! Except you will have my Son's help."

"Samson said, 'Let me die with the Philistines!' Then he pushed with all his might, and down came the temple on the rulers and all the people in it. Thus he killed many more when he died then while he lived."
(Judges 16:30)

So as you look unto the heavens through the eyes and the help of my Son Jesus Christ, the Spirit of my love for you, my chosen one, goes out to you to do his work for you."

"Samson took one last breath, as he pushed with his restored strength of hope in me, the Lord his God! Now, you have been given the breath of life, as you push against the pillars of the temple – the pillars of your life

- as my Son, Jesus Christ helps you push."

"As I see my Son's love for you, I hear his voice that says:

"Jesus called out with a loud voice, 'Father, into your hands I commit my Spirit.' When he had said this, he breathed his last."   *(Luke 23:46)*

"At that moment the curtain of the temple was torn from top to bottom. The earth shook, the rocks split."   *(Matthew 27:51)*

"The temple you were both in came crashing down on you, and my Son, thus killing more enemies - evil spirits - in doing this than you did over your entire life. You feel all the debris hitting you on its way down as you get ready to die underneath all its weight."

"As the dust settles in the aftermath, you realize you are still alive, unlike Samson, who died in his efforts of pushing on the pillars, taking out the enemies in his life. So, you turn to your servant, my Son, Jesus Christ to ask him, 'Why am I still alive?' But he's nowhere to be found! You diligently seek his face, unknowingly acting on my word!

"But without faith it is impossible to please him: for he that cometh to God must believe that he is, and that he is a rewarder of them that diligently seek him."   *(Hebrews 11:6 KJV)*

"You anxiously search for my Son, Jesus Christ, not knowing what had happened to cause his disappearance, until you looked down at your feet. It is then you realized my son Jesus Christ died with all your enemies, as the temple, your life, came crashing down on the both of you; thus sparing your life in order for you to live your life, and live it more abundantly."

"You squat down to see if what you are seeing is real. My son just lies there breathless. You fall to your knees in great sorrow, as you lean onto him to tell him, "I am so sorry, Jesus! Oh my God! I'm sorry God! Please forgive me! Please!"

"Then I say to you, *my child*, my church, and America:

"Beloved, I wish above all things that thou mayest prosper and be in health, <u>EVEN AS THY SOUL PROSPERETH.</u>"   *(3 John 1:2 KJV)*

"The Lord says, 'It was my will that he should suffer. His death was a sacrifice to bring forgiveness. He will see his descendants, he will live a long life, and through him my people will succeed. After a life of suffering, he will know that he did not suffer in vain. My devoted servant, with whom I AM *pleased, will bear the punishment of many and for his sake I will forgive them.'"*   *(Isaiah 53:10-11 GNT)*

MY SON'S PRAYER before his death was:

"I pray that they will all be one, just as you and I are one-as you are in me, Father, and I AM *in you. And may they be in us so that the world will believe you sent me.*

"I have given them the glory you gave me, so they may be one as we are one. I AM *in them and you are in me. May they experience such perfect unity that the world will know that you sent me and that you* love *them as much as you* love *me.*

Father, I want these whom you have given me to be with me where I AM. *Then they can see all the glory you gave me because you* loved *me <u>EVEN BEFORE THE WORLD BEGAN</u>!"*   *(John 17:21-24 NLT)*

America! America! God shed His grace on thee,
And crown thy good with brotherhood
From sea to shining sea!

Thus making you:

ONE NATION, UNDER GOD,
INDIVISIBLE,
WITH LIBERTY,
AND JUSTICE FOR ALL!

In Jesus Christ's name, AMEN!

About the Author

Javier Macias says, "I stand on the authority of the word of God that enables me to see beyond what is seen with the naked eye. Our future is now, Jesus Christ!"

Javier's personal task, and calling, is, "Jesus Christ, and none other!"
He receives messages from God in very unique ways. They can come through a movie, a conversation being carried on by others, a simple gesture made by someone, or a spoken word directly to him from God Himself.

Javier says, "As a servant and Prophet of the Lord, I will not be held accountable unto the Lord for anyone's blood! When called upon to do a work, it must be done with reverence towards the One who called one to do it."

Javier Macias is the founder of, "We Rock Youth Ministries!" We Rock Youth Ministries! is a non-profit, 501(c3) status organization, incorporated in 1999.

We Rock Youth Ministry's foundational faith statement is:

"Therefore if you have any encouragement from being united with Christ, if any comfort from his Love, if any common sharing in the Spirit, if any tenderness and compassion, then make my joy complete by being like minded, having the same Love, being in one Spirit and of one mind.

Do nothing out of selfish ambition or vain conceit. Rather in humility <u>value others above yourselves</u>, not looking to your own interests <u>but each of you to the interest of others.</u> In your relationships with one another, have the <u>SAME MINDSET as Christ Jesus:</u> Who being in very nature God did not consider equality with God something to be used to his own advantage; rather, he made himself nothing by taking the very nature of a servant being made in human likeness. And being found in appearance as a man, he humbled himself by becoming obedient to death- even death on the cross! Therefore God exalted him to the highest place and gave him the name that is above every name, that at the name of Jesus every knee should bow, in heaven and on the earth and under the earth, and <u>EVERY</u> tongue acknowledge that Jesus Christ is Lord, to the glory of God the Father."   *(Philippians 2:1-11,)*

"Look, he is coming with the clouds," and "every eye will see him, even those who pierced him"; and all peoples on earth "will mourn because of him." So shall it be! Amen.

"I AM the Alpha and the Omega," says the Lord God, "who is, and who was, and who is to come, the Almighty."

(Revelation 1:7-8 NIV)

"The word of the Lord came to me, saying, 'Before I formed you in the womb I knew you, before you were born I set you apart; I appointed you as a prophet to the nations.'"   *(Jeremiah 1:4-5)*

"You must speak my words to them, whether they listen or fail to listen, for they are rebellious. But you, son of man, listen to what I say to you. Do not rebel like that rebellious people; open your mouth and eat what I give you." Then I looked, and I saw a hand stretched out to me. In it was a scroll, which he unrolled before me. On both sides of it were written words of lament and mourning and woe."   *(Ezekiel 2:7-10)*

"Son of man, I have made you a watchman for the people of Israel; so hear the word I speak and give them warning from me."   *(Ezekiel 33:7)*
"But if the watchman sees the sword coming and does not blow the

trumpet to warn the people and the sword comes and takes someone's life, that persons life will be taken because of their sin, but I will hold the watchman accountable for their blood." (Ezekiel 33:6)

"Say to them, 'As surely as I live,' declares the Sovereign Lord, 'I take no pleasure in the death of the wicked, but rather that they turn from their ways and live. Turn! Turn from your evil ways! Why will you die, people of Israel?'" (Ezekiel 33:11)

"At this I fell at his feet to worship him. But he said to me, 'Do not do it! I AM a fellow servant with you and with your brothers who hold to the testimony of Jesus. Worship God! For the testimony of Jesus is the Spirit of prophecy.'" (Revelation 19:10)

Sincerely, in Jesus Christ's Love!
Prophet Javier Macias

For Speaking Engagements and
to Contact the Author:
Polly and Javier Macias (254) 227-2348

www.WeRockYouthMinistries.com
werockyouthministries@gmail.com

P.O. Box 242
Groesbeck, TX 76642

www.ingramcontent.com/pod-product-compliance
Lightning Source LLC
Chambersburg PA
CBHW071314040426
42444CB00009B/2013